Spiritual Life on a
Burning Planet

Spiritual Life on a Burning Planet

A Christian Response to Climate Change

DAVID T. BRADFORD

WIPF & STOCK · Eugene, Oregon

SPIRITUAL LIFE ON A BURNING PLANET
A Christian Response to Climate Change

Wipf & Stock
An Imprint of Wipf and Stock Publishers
199 W. 8th Ave., Suite 3
Eugene, OR 97401

www.wipfandstock.com

PAPERBACK ISBN: 978-1-7252-8211-7
HARDCOVER ISBN: 978-1-7252-8212-4
EBOOK ISBN: 978-1-7252-8213-1

Manufactured in the U.S.A.   09/28/20

Contents

Introduction

Then I proceeded to where things were chaotic.

—1 Enoch 21:1

Viewed from outer space, the earth is a blue ball streaked with clouds and mottled with brown. Its speedy rotation and the effect of gravity on its unevenly distributed mass have produced an equatorial bulge. But the earth will look different in coming decades. Heat-induced change in phytoplankton will enhance the color saturation of the oceans' greens and blues.[1] The water will acquire the surreal tonal distortions of digital images on television. Greenland will appear brown and gray as its ice melts and bedrock is exposed. Relieved of the weight of ice, the continent will be displaced and rise a kilometer in height.[2] The textured green of Amazon forests will fade into variegated dullness as the vegetation "transition[s] from high-biomass moist forests to dry forests and woody savannah-like states."[3]

Future changes will not be limited to particular regions; their scope is planetary. "Pervasive ecosystem transformations" are expected, comparable to those that occurred "during the last

1. Dutkiewicz et al., "Ocean Colour," 1–13.

2. Bevins et al., "Bedrock Displacements in Greenland," 1–5.

3. Levine et al., "Ecosystem Heterogeneity," 793. The reported changes are expected to occur "by the end of the 21st century" (793). Also see Oyama and Nobre, "New Climate-Vegetation," 5.1–5.4.

glacial-to-interglacial transformation."[4] With a concerted program of rapid emissions stabilization, the climate worldwide will "move to a state continuously outside the boundary of historical variability" within roughly fifty years.[5] Absent such a program, the shift will occur within about thirty years.[6] These projections are not eccentric. Other scientists have drawn similar conclusions:

> The contemporary climate is moving out of the envelope of Holocene variability, sharply increasing the risk of dangerous climate change. Observations of a climate transition include a rapid retreat of summer sea ice in the Arctic Ocean, retreat of mountain glaciers around the world, loss of mass from the Greenland and West Antarctic ice sheets, an increased rate of sea-level rise in the last 10–15 years, a 4 degrees latitude pole-ward shift of subtropical regions, increased bleaching and mortality in coral reefs, a rise in the number of large floods, and the activation of slow feedback processes like the weakening of the oceanic carbon sink.[7]

None of these changes will be transient, followed by a reversion to historical norms. Ecosystems are retaining the imprints of climate change based on a capacity called ecological memory, "the ability

---

4. Nolan et al., "Past and Future Global Transformation," 920. The trajectory reported in the main text assumes a high-emissions or "business-as-usual" scenario, as we have presently. Glacial-interglacial cycles have waxed and waned for at least 2.6 million years. Apart from the Anthropocene, the cycling pattern has been determined by fluctuations in the earth's orbit and the intensity of solar radiation in the Northern Hemisphere. National Centers for Environmental Information, "Glacial-Interglacial Cycles."

5. Mora et al., "Projected Timing," 183.

6. Mora et al., "Projected Timing," 183. Where I refer to years (fifty, thirty), using 2020 as the baseline, the referenced article uses dates: 2069 (*SD* = 18 years) and 2047 (*SD* = 14 years). I have adjusted for the seven years that have passed since the article's publication in 2013 and also rounded to the nearest decade.

7. Rockström et al., "Planetary Boundaries," art. 32. The Holocene, an interglacial period that began about 11,500 years BP, is the geological epoch that preceded the Anthropocene (National Centers for Environmental Information, "Glacial-Interglacial Cycles").

of the past to influence the present trajectory of ecosystems."[8] "As the time interval shrinks between recurrent shocks, the responses of ecosystems to each new disturbance are increasingly likely to be contingent on the history of other recent extreme events."[9]

Climate change is disturbing natural processes whose duration and field of action surpass our analytical capacity. The projects of sequencing the human genome and travelling to Mars are small efforts compared to grasping and ameliorating the effects of climate change. Natural laws remain in force, but their operation is eluding the predictive powers of human observers. More so in the future, unseen shifts will cause what will appear to be disproportionately major effects. The chaotic orderliness of the Anthropocene has begun.[10]

Earlier periods of climate change were regional in scope, limited in duration, and the outcome of natural cycles.[11] Examples include the Late Antique Ice Age (536–660 CE), which triggered migrations and the invasions of Hun and Germanic tribes that contributed to the fall of the Roman Empire; the Early Medieval Warm Period (950–1200 CE), which saw reduced rainfall and promoted the collapse of the Mayan and Anasazi civilizations; and the Little Ice Age (1300–1700 CE), which chilled Europe and caused flooding, famine, bread riots, and other socioeconomic and environmental upheavals.[12] In their span and deleterious impact, none

8. Hughes et al., "Ecological Memory," 40.

9. Hughes et al., "Ecological Memory," 40.

10. "The Anthropocene is a proposed new geological epoch based on the observation that human impacts on essential planetary processes have become so profound that they have driven the Earth out of the Holocene epoch in which agriculture, sedentary communities, and eventually, socially and technological complex human societies developed" (Steffen et al., "Trajectories of the Earth System," 1). For a historian's discussion of the Anthropocene, see Christian, "Anthropocene Epoch," 339–73.

11. For these cycles and their effects in world history for the period c. 200,000–c. 1,000 BCE, see Fernandez-Armesto, "Farmers' Empire," 106–38; Gamble, "Humanity from the Ice," 13–41; Jones, "Into a Warming World," 71–105.

12. White, *Cold Welcome.*

of these periods measures up to what humans have released in the Anthropocene.

This project is presented in four chapters, entitled Tolling Bells, Burning Planet, Eschatology in the Anthropocene, and The Downward Passage. The first chapter introduces the topic of global warming and outlines some of its biblical and emotional resonances. The ten reviews in the second chapter present what a range of scientists project will be the effects of climate change later in this century. The eight essays in the third chapter address various scriptural, theological, moral, social, and spiritual implications of global warming. Finally, The Downward Passage is concerned with Christ's descent, the Harrowing of Hell, understood as a point of doctrine and an exemplary image of forthcoming challenges as we advance more deeply into the Anthropocene. The chapters differ in style. Tolling Bells is descriptive and occasionally declamatory. Burning Planet is succinct and plain spoken, verging on telegraphic and consistent with reportage. The essays in Eschatology in the Anthropocene are discursively developed arguments. The Downward Passage concludes with a lyrical meditation. At various points, a spiritual path is outlined. Its guiding principle is *penthos*—a process of spiritual transformation that engages contrition and conveys the practitioner through the grief and mourning that signal a true grasp of our having forced the earth into a new geological epoch.

1

Tolling Bells

THE FUTURE IS NOW arriving, its rolling entry signaled in muffled bells and endless news cycles. It peered from Industrial Era dynamos and could be smelled, seen, and touched in the coal-grime streets of Victorian England. It shines from mile-long servers and beams sterile blue light into billions of faces. The eyes of the future are collapsing stars burning through the plasticized surface of political propaganda and media-driven fantasies. An inkling of the facts of climate change cauterizes hope and miniaturizes human aspirations. Those who cower before the facts have accurately gauged their magnitude. At present, the flywheel madness and seeping ingress of chaos is disguised by quotidian semblances of order. But the lord of masks, the loud-shouting god of the Anthropocene, guarantees fleeting crazes and festival routs, all moribund at their point of inception. The sane and safe alternative is to mourn.

The destruction of natural beauty is a grave experience whose poignancy can evolve into rending grief. Bees and tropical butterflies are becoming *memento mori*.[1] The bodies of migratory

---

1. Koh et al., "Co-Extinctions of Tropical Butterflies," 272–74; Sánchez-Bayo and Wyckhuys, "Worldwide Decline," 8–27.

birds are shrinking.[2] Icecaps are disappearing, and boreal forests are burning. Extreme weather is disrupting the predictable continuity of outdoor time. Seasonal changes are becoming less clearly marked. An uncanny change is underway, its scope exceeding our power of imagination. Tides of anxiety and sadness can be expected, passing among individuals and saturating crowds. Bourgeois urbanites whose exposure to the natural world is limited to worms in organic tomatoes will be among the last to react. Confused and lonely, they will feel haunted by their devices and the muted clatter of their silver kitchen implements. Another predictable response is fear, of such intensity that it grades into nausea and progresses toward a palpable silence that tips into panic. Repeated episodes of panic will erode what hope and confidence remain, at which point the fear becomes despair. Fomented in large groups, the emotions aroused by the malign effects of climate change will reverse polarity and prompt outrage and upheavals of violence. Climate change is physical at base, but its psychological effects will prove pervasively disturbing. Many will seek solace in the virtual world, their minds fixed in chronic states of addictive hypnosis. A worldwide lament, paired with ubiquitous acts of penitence, would create a slim chance of mounting sufficient courage and moral imagination to alter our self-determined fate. Even then, the material processes that are already in motion would be impossible to stop.

Conclusive data are now arriving. The evolutionary experiment of human consciousness is drawing toward its completion. The imposing drama of human advance has proved itself a dumb tragedy of self-sacrifice in which the victors are destroying their homes. The drama did not begin with faulty moral judgement— "knowing what is good and what is bad"—nor with actions as mundane as sex—"they realized that they were naked" (Gen 3:5, 7). The actors' gender difference is irrelevant; they were two-in-one, "the most cunning of all the animals" (Gen 3:1). Eve presented the fruit to Adam, but both received the message of warning. Adam's self-incriminating pretense of ignorance is the tactic of blaming the victim: "she gave me the fruit—so I ate it" (Gen 3:12). The thematic

2. Weeks et al., "Shared Morphological Consequences."

axis of the drama runs vertically through the tree situated in the "middle of the garden" (Gen 3:3). Other trees were lush and unforbidden but not centrally located. The first act of the drama is the bent-heart action of idolatry—of oneself and one's kind. What followed shows the cost of usurping the center in the effort to "be like gods" (Gen 3:5). The second act was the couple's expulsion and exile: "What have you done! Listen: Cursed be the ground because of you!" (Gen 3:17). They were expelled and "banned," their return prevented by a "fiery revolving sword" (Gen 3:14, 24). Life thereafter entailed "toiling" and "crawling" (Gen 3:14, 17). The third act of the drama was a murder: Cain killing Abel: "Your brother's blood cries out to me from the soil" (Gen 4:10). So began our fitful travels in widening arcs from an imaginary home. We are "restless wanderers" and kin to Cain, a mongrel species since departing the African homeland (Gen 4:12).[3] Now we are turning in circles as the earth becomes increasingly strange. We have made ourselves resident aliens on a burning planet.

The Christian narrative of salvation history deviates from today's developing scenarios of global warming.[4] The viability of its plan necessitates physical circumstances the world has known for millennia. But the earth is changing—to the extent that its future may not be habitable. We have put the plan into doubt. The tiered, supernaturally inflected world of ancient times may have folded into the empirical world of modern astronomy and physics; but the

3. The phrase "mongrel species" and the emphasis on migration are based on Reich, *Who We Are*.

4. Scholarly perspectives on *salvation history* (*Heilsgeschichte*) range from classic, biblically oriented formulations (as in Gerhard von Rad's "fundamental conception of history as a continuum of events determined by Jahweh's promise") to recent post-modern views in which the constancy of religious meaning across historical time is denied (von Rad, *Old Testament Theology*, 426). In setting the Christian narrative of salvation history against the facts of climate change, the point is that *all* such perspectives come to nothing under certain scenarios of future warming. This is clearly the case in Hothouse Earth pathways, as discussed in later chapters, and it also applies to lesser threats in which warming-induced socioeconomic changes lead to the decay of civil society and the collapse of expansive, expensively maintained institutions. The church (since Constantine) is such an institution. For critical consideration of varied concepts of salvation history, see Hinze, "End of Salvation History."

difference in cosmology hardly matters. High civilization and, possibly, humankind are precarious. Given these circumstances, shall we allow God a freedom that He permits His creatures: the freedom to withdraw from promises to which He previously adhered? Amos promoted this option more so than other prophets.[5] He allowed God the freedom that God allows His creatures: the freedom to retreat, to cancel, to withdraw. Opportunities were offered, then encapsulated in the Incarnation, and now their material foundation—a habitable earth—is deteriorating at the hands of those to whom the opportunities were offered. The branches are being stripped, the rootstock is smoldering. Is there hope? For institutions and large social collectives as we now know them—no. For earth in the form that has served humans for millennia—no. For spiritually avid persons and their remnant bands—yes.[6]

5. For Amos's distinctiveness in this respect, see Hasel, *Remnant*.

6. For remnant theology in Jewish scripture, through Isaiah, see Hasel, *Remnant*. For the remnant in Zephaniah, see King, "Remnant in Zephaniah," 414–27.

2

Burning Planet

THE FIRST OF THE following reviews is a brief introduction to the science of climate change. The goal of the remaining reviews is to create a sweeping, pointillist sense of the effects of climate change on human life, particularly after mid-century. Technical terms have been kept to a minimum. Numbers must be used to indicate temperature, but calculations, mathematical formulas, and statistical procedures are avoided. The substance of the reviews is based entirely on empirical research. No one review provides complete coverage of its topic, nor is the gathering of reviews here comprehensive. The reviews are meant to be reasonable and moderate in tone rather than alarmist. Any sense of catastrophe they convey is inherent in the facts reported.

The topics are highly varied—ranging from rising seas and extreme weather to urbanization and mass extinction. Climate change sets dominoes into motion; some converge at points remote from changing weather. The relationship of extreme weather, urbanization, and pandemic disease is a relatively clear-cut example. As drought destroys the economic base in their home countries, many people will migrate to large cities, which are prime incubation sites for new strains of virus. Lengthier coverage is granted to topics least likely to be familiar to lay readers. For example, extreme weather events are addressed in passing, while ecological grief is discussed at length.

CLIMATE SCIENCE

The 2015 Paris Agreement, released by the Intergovernmental Panel on Climate Change (IPCC), calls for "holding the increase in the global average temperature to well below 2°C above pre-industrial levels and pursuing efforts to limit the temperature increase to 1.5°C above pre-industrial levels."[1] Throughout the literature, the standard of comparison when measuring a rise in the global mean temperature is the *preindustrial level*. This baseline can be determined in different ways; none is a perfect fit for all studies. The mean temperature during the period from 1720 to 1800, for example, has certain advantages because the "natural factors that affect Earth's climate—the levels of solar and volcanic activity—were both at similar levels" during this period as they are today; thus, any deviation from the mean temperature since then would represent anthropogenic effects.[2]

The predictive models and data sets used for the Paris Agreement are now regarded as relatively uninformed, making its proposed trajectories and target temperatures either outdated or overly optimistic. The mean global temperature reached 1.0°C above the preindustrial level in 2015; under current policies, the rise is likely to exceed 1.5°C before midcentury and may hit 3.2°C by 2100.[3] Even if all nations met their Paris commitments, the temperature rise may reach "at least 3°C of global warming," or (as predicted in another study), 2.9°C by midcentury.[4] The IPCC report mentions the possibly of our breaching the 1.5°C threshold by 2040; more current predictions give the date as 2030, our then breaking

---

1. United Nations Framework Convention on Climate Change, *Report of the Conference.*

2. Hawkins et al., "Estimating Changes," 1.

3. Climate Action Tracker, "Pledged Action."

4. Lenton et al., "Climate Tipping Points," 592; Climate Action Tracker, "Pledged Action."

the 2.0°C mark by 2045 (with a 10 percent chance of doing so by 2025).[5] A 2014 summary review of three hundred predictive scenarios concludes: "Baseline scenarios, those without additional mitigation, result in global mean surface temperature increases in 2100 from 3.7°C to 4.8°C compared to pre-industrial levels."[6] To put these data in perspective, "the Greenland ice sheet could be doomed at 1.5°C of warming, which could occur as soon as 2030."[7] It appears that the 1.5°C limit recommended in the Paris Agreement is practically impossible to achieve and that the goal of holding warming to well below 2.0°C above the preindustrial level is little more than aspirational.

Yet greater temperature rises have been predicted, based on addressing factors that previous research did not identify or adequately emphasize. For example, and granted "the absence of any climate policy," "the median surface warming in 2091–2100" could range from 5.0°C to 7.0°C above the preindustrial level.[8] "It is widely agreed that warmings of over 6°C would have disastrous consequences for humankind."[9] In scenarios of this nature, identified as "Hothouse Earth" pathways, some or most of the settled world becomes uninhabitable due to the risk of heat stress:

> We conclude that a global-mean warming of roughly 7°C would create small zones where metabolic heat dissipation would for the first time become impossible, calling into question their suitability for human habitation. A warming of 11 to 12°C would expand these zones to encompass most of today's human population.[10]

5. Xu et al., "Global Warming," 30–32.

6. When "climate uncertainties" are taken into account, the range is 2.5°C to 7.8°C (Edenhofer et al., "IPCC, 2014").

7. Lenton et al., "Climate Tipping Points," 592.

8. Sokolov et al., "Probabilistic Forecast," 5175–204. Also see Lenton et al., "Climate Tipping Points"; Steffen et al., "Trajectories"; Xu et al., "Global Warming."

9. Sherwood and Huber, "Adaptability Limit," 9552.

10. Sherwood and Huber, "Adaptability Limit." A person could not simply move from a warmer to a cooler area with the assumption that all would then be well: "Peak potential heat stress is surprisingly similar across many regions on Earth" (9553).

Importantly, the rise in mean global temperature would not have to reach such high levels before serious consequences ensue: "Significant risks of deleterious climate impacts for society and the environment have to be faced even if the 2°C line can be held."[11] "If the Paris Accord target of a 1.5°C–2.0°C rise in temperature is met, we cannot exclude the risk that a cascade of reactions could push the Earth System irreversibly onto a 'Hothouse Earth' pathway."[12]

The sampled predictions span a range of outcomes, the most extreme of which naturally draws attention and provokes alarm. But those at the "good" end of the spectrum—such as 2.0°C—also imply serious prospects. The breadth of the range of predictions does not reflect "bad science," but rather the complexity of the factors in play and the moral status of our future decision-making. Few studies project beyond the year 2100; countless unknowns complicate predictions at such a distance.[13] But "warming will not stop in 2100 if emissions continue," as they are, indeed, continuing, reaching ever-higher levels.[14] Atmospheric CO_2 "is rapidly heading towards levels last seen 50 million years ago—in the Eocene—when temperatures were up to 14°C higher than they were in pre-industrial times."[15]

The patterns of causal relations within and across climatic systems are exceedingly complex. Key terms in the literature suggest as much: *tipping point* (the onset of a large-scale discontinuity); *resilience* (inherent restorative capacity); *self-regulation* (the monitoring and regulative functions of a system); *threshold effect* (when the

11. Rockström et al., "Planetary Boundaries," 32.

12. Steffen at al., "Trajectories," 8254. Deadly combinations of heat and humidity are already being reported by weather stations in certain subtropical locations (Raymond et al., "Emergence of Heat," 1–8).

13. Pathways through the year 2100 are modeled as *Representative Concentration Pathways* (RCPs). *Extended Concentration Pathways* (ECPs) track the "possible development trajectories for the main forcing agents of climate change" through the year 2300 (van Vuuren et al., "Representative Concentration," 7).

14. Sherwood and Huber, "Adaptability Limit," 9552. For the ongoing increase in carbon emissions, see Friedlingstein et al., "Global Carbon Budget 2019."

15. Lenton et al., "Climate Tipping Points," 595.

incremental build-up of lesser effects anticipates and encourages a sudden, relatively extreme change); and *cascade* (when converging effects prompt the occurrence of an array of powerful, possibly unpredicted effects). These concepts are used in combination to assess the present status of a system and predict future scenarios. For example, a loss of resilience in the component systems of a larger system hastens its rate of deteriorative change, possibly nudging the system to a tipping point and subsequent collapse. "Dramatic demographic collapses of resource-strapped societies" have been interpreted on this basis, and the same reasoning applies on larger, even global scales.[16]

Extreme climate hazards, such as "warming, heatwaves, precipitation, drought, floods, fires, storms, sea-level rise and changes in natural land cover and ocean chemistry," are predicted to occur not only more frequently as this century advances, but also more often in converging patterns and within limited time frames.[17] "By 2100, the world's population will be exposed concurrently to the equivalent of the largest magnitude in one of these hazards if emissions are aggressively reduced, or three if they are not, with some tropical coastal areas facing up to six simultaneous hazards."[18]

Causal frameworks based on one-to-one linear effects operating within individual systems cannot begin to capture the complex patterns of causation within and across climatic systems. The following examples, all concerned with a half-degree rise from 1.5°C to 2.0°C, illustrate warming's effect on coral reefs, agriculture, and freshwater resources.[19] Notice that the reported changes reflect nonlinear transitions. Coral reefs may reverse some of their previous die-off were the temperature rise kept to 1.5°C, but would be destroyed at 2.0°C. Freshwater resources in the Mediterranean basin will fall 9 percent at 1.5°C, but this figure is nearly doubled at 2.0°C. Wheat and soy farming at higher latitudes may show improvement at 1.5°C (due to elevated atmospheric carbon dioxide

---

16. Scheffer, "Anticipating Societal Collapse"; also see Carpenter et al., "Dancing on the Volcano."

17. Mora et al., "Broad Threat to Humanity," 1062.

18. Mora et al., "Broad Threat to Humanity," 1062.

19. Silberg, "Why a Half-Degree Temperature Rise Is a Big Deal."

in relatively cooler geographic areas); but at 2.0°, the advantage falls by 700 percent for soy and disappears for wheat. Food plants have their respective thermal limits, beyond which their growth is harmed. For example, corn may thrive under warmer conditions until the cob fails to develop because the increased heat prevents later stages of growth.

The geographic scope of some climatic systems is immense. Consider the consequences of global warming on the dominant currents within the Atlantic Ocean, which combine to form the Atlantic Meridional Overturning Circulation:

> Arctic warming and Greenland melting are driving an influx of fresh water into the North Atlantic. This could have contributed to a 15 percent slowdown since the mid-twentieth century of the Atlantic Meridional Over- turning Circulation (AMOC), a key part of global heat and salt transport by the ocean. Rapid melting of the Greenland ice sheet and further slowdown of the AMOC could destabilize the West African monsoon, trigger- ing drought in Africa's Sahel region. A slowdown in the AMOC could also dry the Amazon, disrupt the East Asian monsoon and cause heat to build up in the South- ern Ocean, which could accelerate Antarctic ice loss.[20]

Other changes, geographically peripheral to those described but related to Atlantic circulation, include harm to the boreal forests in North America and Siberia and the thawing of permafrost in both areas.

The research techniques available to climate scientists have become far more sensitive and data-enriched over the past few de- cades. Readings of dropping barometric pressure before the disas- trous 1901 Galveston hurricane are like Paleolithic cave scratching compared to the modeling and data-gathering procedures available in present-day climate science. Such models can account for both physical observations and a variety of demographic and socioeco- nomic variables. On this basis, numerical and narrative scenarios are developed, representing different global trajectories, each

20. Lenton et al., "Climate Tipping Points," 594.

serving as a baseline for the prediction of possible future outcomes. For example, the *Shared Socioeconomic Pathways* framework provides five narratives, ranging from one in which mitigation and adaptation to warming are managed effectively ("Sustainability—Taking the Green Road"), to another pathway in which mitigation and adaptation are low priorities and hard to achieve ("Regional Rivalry—A Rocky Road").[21] The latter pathway is the more disastrous and reflects our present direction, certainly under the present administration in the United States.

In creating a comprehensive account of climate change, inclusive of the entire Earth System, scientists affiliated with the Stockholm Resilience Centre have identified nine *planetary boundaries.* A boundary is an outside limit, beyond which the Earth System moves into deep jeopardy. Trespassing a boundary leads to "serious disruptions of ecosystems, society, and economies."[22] Each boundary pertains to adverse effects in a particular natural system; examples include biodiversity loss, ocean acidification, and atmospheric aerosol loading. The climate itself is only one such system and densely interactive with the others. "Planetary boundaries are interdependent, because transgressing one may both shift the position of other boundaries or cause them to be transgressed."[23] We have irreversibly trespassed three boundaries; two others have probably been trespassed; and the data needed to quantify three additional boundaries are presently lacking.

Climate change has been demonstrated by "a very robust evidence base" and invites "almost no disagreement" in scientific circles.[24] We are responsible; this is old news.[25] The detection of

21. The pathways defined by physical observations are called *Representative Concentration Pathways* (RCPs). For Shared Socioeconomic Pathways (SSPs) and the RCPs, see Hausfather, "Climate Modeler Explainer"; Riahi "Shared Socioeconomic Pathways," 153–68.

22. Rockström et al., "Planetary Boundaries," 32. Also see Steffen et al., "Planetary Boundaries," 1–10.

23. Rockström et al., "Planetary Boundaries," 32.

24. UN Environment, *Global Environment Outlook*, 4.

25. The Swedish chemist Svante Arrhenius published the first calculation of global warming resulting from human emissions of CO_2 in 1896. For a

global warming has become fine-grained and is no longer limited to regional trends developing over decades and centuries. "Research now finds that a human influence is discernible on global patterns of daily temperature and moisture."[26] Our influence is detectable on any given day: "The fingerprint of climate change is detected from any single day in the observed global record since 2012, and since 1999 on the basis of a year of data."[27]

Recent observations show that the world is warming at an accelerating speed.[28] The time lost for mitigation is a serious matter: "The lower the stabilization level (for emissions) and the longer the delay, the higher are the additional costs of mitigation and the more difficult, or even unfeasible, it will become to keep global warming low."[29] The lost decades have created a whirlwind of biblical proportions, a war-horse whose "frenzied excitement eats up the ground" (Job 39:24). Notably, minimizing or even halting warming is not a cure-all for its future consequences. Inevitably, forces already in motion will ramify into countless points of future impact. For example, the oceans would not cool quickly were rising air temperature halted. Oceans are thermal sinks; pack ice will melt from underneath. Florida may disappear from the map within a few centuries regardless of how soon air temperature begins to cool.[30] Mitigation strategies, including geoengineering solutions, have been proposed; few have been adequately tested or proven safe, effective, and affordable.[31] The moral problems surrounding

chronological survey of key developments in climate science, see Weart, "Discovery of Global Warming." In the United States, political expediency and corporate avarice have been responsible for delays in addressing global warming (Banerjee et al., *Exxon*; Rich, *Losing the Earth*).

26. Min, "Human Fingerprint," 15.

27. Sippel et al., "Climate Change Now Detectable," 35.

28. Forster et al., "Latest Models," 7–10.

29. Climate Policy Info Hub, "Costs of Mitigation."

30. Silberg, "Why a Half-Degree Temperature Rise Is a Big Deal."

31. "Current climate engineering proposals do not come close to addressing the complex and contested nature of conceivable 'climate emergencies' resulting from unabated greenhouse-gas emissions" (Sillmann et al., "Climate Emergencies," 290). For a review of geoengineering strategies, see Natural Environment Research Council, "Experiment Earth."

the engineering strategies create a dark nimbus, impenetrable apart from highly cultivated religious perspectives.

WARMING

A wide latitudinal band of the earth's surface spanning Africa, Asia, and the Near and Middle East is becoming uninhabitable due to warming. Within a few decades, those working outdoors in these areas may die of heat stress; even nighttime temperatures will threaten the health of children, the old, the infirm. The human toll of warming is becoming apparent; in 2015, for example, heat waves in India and Pakistan contributed to 4,500 deaths.[32] This band is fraught with terrorism and famine, but rich in mineral deposits. Inhabitants in these areas are dying of starvation, contagious disease, and warfare, and will do so at higher rates with the added scourge of hyperthermia.[33] Intolerable conditions in their home countries will force populations to migrate into first-world countries, increasing their economic burden and testing their frayed remnants of civil behavior.

The modeling procedure called *climate-analog mapping* predicts the future climate of cities in North America based on their likeness to the existing climates of present-day cities.[34] Anticipated changes are set to occur later this century and generally represent shifts to the south and west, to areas that are, at present, warmer and dryer. Washington, DC, will have the climate of a town in the Ozark forests of central Arkansas. Austin, Texas, will have the desert climate of a Mexican town hundreds of miles to the southwest. The future climate of some cites is so deviant as to have no climate analogs in present-day North America.

32. ClimaticAnalytics, "Global Warming."

33. Brown and Crawford, *Rising Temperatures;* Burke et al., "Warming Increases," 20674; Klein, "Let Them Drown," 11–14.

34. Fitzpatrick and Dunn, "Contemporary Climatic Analogs," 1–7.

RISING SEAS

Approximately 13 percent of the earth's surface is melting. This is the cryosphere, the "frozen components of the Earth System."[35] Much of the melted water passes into the sea, particularly from Antarctica and Greenland, where most of the world's freshwater has been locked in place. A sea-level rise of one to two meters is predicted to occur by 2100.[36] Flooding and storm surges near ever-shrinking coastlines will increase accordingly. "Extreme sea level events that are historically rare (once per century in the recent past) are projected to occur more frequently (at least once per year) in many locations by 2050."[37] Millions of people are threatened by rising seas. "The low-lying coastal zone is currently home to around 680 million people (nearly 10% of the 2010 global population), and is projected to reach more than one billion by 2050."[38] Displaced persons, forming "waves of climate migrants," will "reshape the population distribution" in many countries.[39]

RISING COSTS

The financial burden of protecting against rising seas and compensating for other climate-related disasters is astronomical.[40] "Unmitigated warming is expected to reshape the global economy by reducing average global incomes roughly 23%" by 2100.[41] The

35. Pörtner et al., "IPCC, 2019," 2.

36. Horton et al., "Estimating"; Wuebbles et al., "Executive Summary," 12–34.

37. Pörtner et al., "IPCC, 2019," 42. The parenthetical material is part of the original quotation. In New York City, for example, "100-year surge flooding is to occur at intervals of 3–20 years by the end of this century" (Lin et al., "Physically Based Assessment," 462).

38. Pörtner et al., "IPCC, 2019," 42. The parenthetical material is part of the original quotation.

39. Hauer, "'Migration Induced by Sea-Level Rise," 324. For displacement, flooding, and storm surges, also see World Meteorological Organization, *WMO Statement,* 29–33.

40. Ackerman and Stanton, *Cost of Climate Change.*

41. Burke et al., "Global Non-Linear Effect," 235.

ratio of public debt to gross domestic product is expected to double due to an increased frequency of banking crises, with the annual fiscal burden representing 5 to 15 percent of gross domestic product. About "20% of these effects are caused by the deterioration of banks' balance sheets induced by climate change."[42]

A study specific to the United States showed "complex patterns of projected changes across the country, with damages in some sectors (for example, labour, extreme temperature mortality, and coastal property) estimated to range in the hundreds of billions of US dollars annually by the end of the century under high emissions."[43] The scope of the financial damage is such that "no regions escape some mix of adverse impacts."[44]

EXTREME WEATHER

Extreme weather is unseasonal and severe, a deviation from expectations based on historical norms. Heat waves, cold waves, and drought as well as tropical cyclones and extreme precipitation events will all increase in frequency and intensity as climate change advances.[45] Extreme weather events "have occurred throughout history—but previous benchmarks are no longer valid; 1-in-100-year events are happening more often, and their timescales are shortening."[46]

Satellite images from the summer of 2017 show the highly unusual occurrence of three hurricanes spinning simultaneously

42. Lamperti et al., "Public Costs," 829.

43. Martinich and Crimmins, "Climate Damages," 397–404.

44. Martinich and Crimmins, "Climate Damages," 397–404.

45. *Tropical cyclone* is the general term for "a rotating, organized system of clouds and thunderstorms that originates over tropical or subtropical waters and has a closed, low-level circulation" (NOAA, "What is the Difference between a Hurricane and a Typhoon"). A cyclone that forms in the North Atlantic, central North Pacific, or eastern North Pacific is a *hurricane,* and one that forms in the Northwest Pacific is a *typhoon.* A comparable weather system, regardless of strength, that forms in the South Pacific or the Indian Ocean is a *tropical storm.*

46. Nature Climate Change, "Storms Ahead," 671.

in the Atlantic basin. In warming the seas and melting polar ice, climate change is reducing the earth's albedo, its capacity to reflect solar radiation.[47] An inevitable consequence is already apparent: hurricanes of greater intensity in the Atlantic basin, and increases in the intensity and frequency of typhoons and tropical storms in the Indian and western Pacific oceans.[48] The "translation speed" of these powerful atmospheric systems—their speed of advance across the earth's surface—is slowing, with their "sluggish movement substantially increasing the risk of life and destruction."[49] Not only is their speed lessening, amplifying their ferocity at landfall; they are also becoming wetter, delivering more precipitation, and will increasingly be followed by heat waves.[50]

STARVATION

The nutritional value of food crops will be reduced as atmospheric CO_2 rises to levels predicted within the next thirty to eighty years.[51] Protein, iron, and zinc will be affected, also the vitamins B1, B2, B5, and B9.[52] "For the current century, estimates of the potential human health impact for these declines range from 138 million to 1.4 billion (people), depending on the nutrient."[53] Those bearing the brunt of these changes live in the Middle East and the Global South—Africa and South and Southeast Asia. Consider the two billion people who live where the primary food source is rice, and the consequences for children and women of childbearing age who live in countries where the prevalence of anemia is already 20 percent. Serious attempts to address the problem are unlikely to produce

47. Riihela et al., "Observed Changes," 895–98.

48. Geophysical Fluid Dynamics Laboratory, "Global Warming and Hurricanes."

49. Simpkins, "Cyclones Slow Down," 104.

50. For increased wetness, see Center for Climate and Energy Solutions, "Climate Basics." For the sequence of tropical cyclones followed by heat waves, see Lin, "Tropical Cyclones and Heatwaves," 579–80.

51. Smith and Meyers, "Impact of Anthropogenic CO2 Emissions," 834–39.

52. Zhu Xu et al., "Carbon Dioxide (CO2) Levels," 1.

53. Zhu Xu et al., "Carbon Dioxide (CO2) Levels," 1.

solutions, because the economic burden of stringent mitigation will only compound the problem of hunger: "A robust finding is that by 2050, stringent climate mitigation policy, if implemented evenly across all sectors and regions, would have a greater negative impact on global hunger and food consumption than the direct impacts of climate change."[54] This catch-22 is one of many in the literature on mitigation. The prevailing message is that we are approaching—if we have not already surpassed—certain limits that render aggressive mitigation counterproductive.

Food production accounts for 50 percent of the earth's habitable land; of what remains, 37 percent is covered by forests and the rest by cities and freshwater.[55] The practice of cutting and burning equatorial forests for purposes of mining and farming is destroying important carbon sinks. Even now, due to deforestation and the disturbance of forested land, tropical forests are a net carbon source: "Carbon losses exceed gain on every continent."[56] New seeds will probably be developed, and farming may improve in parts of the northern hemisphere, but freshwater resources are in decline and dead zones in oceans and large lakes are expanding.[57]

POLLUTION

Pollution "is the largest environmental cause of disease and premature death."[58] Its principle causes are industrial and farming practices that also promote warming. What follows concerns air pollution: four thousand Chinese die annually from air pollution, and as many as two hundred thousand Americans die prematurely on the same basis.[59] "Air pollution is the main environmental contributor

---

54. Hasegawa et al., "Risk of Food Insecurity," 699.

55. UN Environment, *Global Environment Outlook.*

56. Baccini et al., "Tropical Forests," 230.

57. Ripple et al., "'World Scientists' Warning to Humanity," 1026–28. This article has 1,500 signatories. For "dead zones" resulting from warming, deoxygenation, and agricultural run-off, see Laffoley and Baxter, *Ocean Deoxygenation.*

58. Landrigan et al., "Lancet Commission," 462.

59. Smedley, *Clearing the Air.*

to the global burden of disease, leading to between 6 million and 7 million premature deaths and welfare losses estimated at US$5 trillion annually."[60] Ninety-one percent of the global population lives in areas in which the air quality exceeds internationally sanctioned safety standards.[61] The gasses and particulates that harm these people trap heat and increase warming. Among other adverse effects, long-term exposure to air pollution causes cognitive impairment, particularly among the elderly.[62] The incidence of environmentally induced dementia will rise accordingly.

POPULATION

The population of the world is now at 7.7 billion and "could grow to 8.5 billion in 2030, 9.7 billion in 2050, and 10.9 billion in 2100."[63] The population at present may already exceed the earth's carrying capacity, the maximum number it can sustain over time.[64] Significantly, none of these future population estimates accounts for global warming's adverse effects on agriculture.

The number of persons age sixty or older is expected to double by 2050, reaching 2.1 billion, and is likely to triple by 2100, reaching 3.1 billion.[65] In 2018, for the first time in history, persons age sixty-five or older outnumbered children below age five. By 2050, the number of persons age sixty-five or older is likely to surpass the number of adolescents and young adults age fifteen to twenty-four.[66]

60. UN Environment, *Global Environment Outlook*, 7.

61. World Health Organization, *Ambient Air Pollution*.

62. Zhang et al., "Impact of Exposure," 9193–97; National Institute of Environmental Health Science, "Air Pollution."

63. United Nations Department of Economic and Social Affairs, *Population Prospects 2019*.

64. United Nations Department of Economic and Social Affairs, "World Population"; also see UNEP Global Environmental Alert Service, "One Planet, How Many People?"

65. United Nations Department of Economic and Social Affairs, Population Division, *World Population Ageing 2017*; for demographic patterns in global ageing, see Palacios, "Future of Global Ageing."

66. United Nations Department of Economic and Social Affairs, *World*

At that point, one-third of the global population may be unfit to work. Consider the elderly at mid-century and beyond: idling in the gloom, coughing tawny air, perched in dim windows like owls in desolate places.

URBANIZATION

In 2017, 50 percent of the global population lived in cities, and in 2050, 68 percent will do so.[67] In 2014, there were twenty-eight megacities, each with a population exceeding ten million people. Twelve additional megacities are projected for 2030. At present, the number of displaced persons is 70.8 million, many of whom will settle in megacities.[68] One-sixth of the population in megacities lives in slums, near open sewers and garbage; one-sixth now, but many more later, as the economic base in rural areas yields to the damaging effects of warming. Meanwhile, socioeconomic stratification will shunt millions more to the bottom of urban heaps, amplifying the risk of urban uprisings that evolve into regional wars.[69]

Cities produce 70 percent of global CO_2 emissions. The percentage will rise, as will the waste, which now measures 1.3 billion tons annually.[70] "Some 2.3 billion people (approximately 1 in 3 of the global population) still lack access to safe sanitation."[71] At present, 1.4 million people die each year from preventable disease due to "pathogen-polluted drinking water and inadequate sanitation."[72]

Population Prospects 2019.

67. United Nations Department of Economic and Social Affairs, *World Urbanization Prospects 2018.*

68. UN Refugee Agency, *Global Trends.*

69. For the role of socioeconomic disparity in precipitating world wars, see Scheidel, *Great Leveler.* Optimistic views about decreasing human violence do not account for the socioeconomic consequences of climate change (e.g., Pinker, *Better Angels of Our Nature*).

70. Population Connection, "Urbanization and the Megacity."

71. UN Environment, *Global Environment Outlook,* 12. The parenthetical material is part of the original quotation.

72. UN Environment, *Global Environment Outlook,* 12.

The number is bound to increase. Megacities are prime incubation sites for strains of influenza and as yet unidentified viruses.[73]

MASS EXTINCTION

The sixth mass extinction is under way—"the first to be driven specifically by the impacts of human activities on the planet."[74] Several species of vertebrates become extinct each year in the natural course of events. Five hundred have become extinct within the past century, which is one hundred times higher than the background rate.[75] Fifty percent of vertebrate species are likely to become extinct by mid-century, and 40 percent of insect species within the next few decades.[76] "Since the advent of the Anthropocene, humans have increased the rate of species extinction by 100 to 1,000 times the background rates that were typical over Earth's history."[77]

Reductions in the density and diversity of biological life can occur in nonlinear ways. With an abnormal change in its thermal niche, an entire biological community can collapse abruptly, "transforming the ecosystem state and the goods and services it provides."[78] Such abrupt changes, known as *regime shifts*, "occur over 'human' timescales of years and decades, meaning the collapse of large vulnerable ecosystems, such as the Amazon rainforest and Caribbean coral reefs, may take only a few decades once triggered."[79] Abrupt changes of this nature have been observed in marine environments since the 1980s; another such transformation

73. Butler, "Infectious Disease Emergence," 1–5.

74. Rockström et al., "Planetary Boundaries," 32; Ceballos et al., "Biological Annihilation," 8.

75. Leadley et al., *Biodiversity Scenarios;* Thomas et al., "Extinction Risk from Climate Change," 145–48.

76. Sanchez-Bayo and Wyckhuys, "Worldwide Decline," 8–27.

77. Rockström et al., "Planetary Boundaries," 40.

78. Beaugrand et al., "Prediction of Unprecedented Biological Shifts," 237.

79. Cooper et al., "Regime Shifts." Such shifts occur disproportionately faster in large ecosystems compared with smaller ones: "Each additional unit area of an ecosystem provides an increasingly smaller unit of time taken for that system to collapse."

"is predicted after 2014—unprecedented in its magnitude and extent—coinciding with a strong El Nino event and major shifts in Northern Hemisphere climate."[80] More generally, "anthropogenic pressures on the Earth System have reached a scale where abrupt global environmental change can no longer be excluded."[81] A 2005 survey among more than 1,300 scientists "concluded that changes to ecosystems due to human activities were more rapid in the past 50 years than at any time in human history, increasing the risks of abrupt and irreversible changes."[82]

Not only are animals, insects, and plants succumbing to climate change; humans may find their adaptive skills tested beyond their capacity as the world changes around them.

SUICIDE

Over the past three decades, global warming has contributed to nearly sixty thousand suicides in India.[83] Unfettered climate change "could result in 9–40,000 additional suicides . . . in the United States and Mexico by 2050."[84] Suicide rates vary systematically with climatic conditions, and the association "is similar in hotter versus cooler regions and has not diminished over time, indicating limited historical adaptation."[85] Because the association is systematic and reliably present across both cooler and warmer regions, heat is not the only decisive factor. Ongoing, relatively higher ambient temperatures, paired with detrimental changes in the body's cooling capacity due to environmental humidity, disturb the internal thermal milieu, which is constrained by nature and controlled by the hypothalamus.[86] Possible results range from

80. Beaugrand et al., "Prediction of Unprecedented Biological Shifts," 237.

81. Rockström et al., 'Planetary Boundaries."

82. Stockholm Resilience Centre, "Nine Planetary Boundaries." For the article on which this summary is based, see Steffen et al., "Planetary Boundaries."

83. Carleton, "Crop-Damaging Temperatures," 8746–51.

84. Burke et al., "Higher Temperatures," 723.

85. Burke et al., "Higher Temperatures," 723.

86. For thermal regulation, see: Zhao et al., "Hypothalamic Circuit that

physical discomfort and emotional disturbance to delirium, coma, organ failure, and death.

Since the mid-Holocene, when settled urban life began about six thousand years ago, "human populations have resided in the same narrow part of the climatic envelope . . . , characterized by a major mode around ~11°C to 15°C mean annual temperature."[87] Crops and livestock are similarly limited, "and the same optimum [temperature range] has been found for agricultural and nonagricultural economic output" in both ancient and modern societies.[88] Within fifty years, depending on future warming and population growth, "1 to 3 billion people are projected to be left outside the climate conditions that have served humanity well over the past 6,000 years."[89] We are altering our climatic niche, destroying the envelope that shields our species, and we are killing ourselves in greater number as we do so.

ECOLOGICAL GRIEF

Nature Climate Change, a prestigious scientific journal, has devoted an entire issue to the psychopathology that results from living in deteriorating natural environments.[90] Professional societies, recognizing the risk to public health posed by climate change, have made the recommendation that we plan for future needs—the psychological needs of virtually the entire population of the world.[91]

Climate change has varied psychological effects. Some are traumatic, as follow in the wake of surviving a single natural

---

Controls Body Temperature," 2042–47. For the interaction of heat and humidity (and the related term *wet-bulb temperature*), see Sherwood and Huber, "Adaptability Limit," 9552–55; Raymond et al., "Emergence of Heat and Humidity," 1–8.

87. The mean annual temperature of this envelope is ~13°C. See Xu et al., "Future of the Human Climate Niche," 1.

88. See Xu et al., "Future of the Human Climate Niche," 1.

89. See Xu et al., "Future of the Human Climate Niche," 1.

90. Nature Climate Change, "Focusing on Climate Change," 8.

91. Bourque and Cunsolo Willox, "Climate Change," 415–22; Clayton et al., *Mental Health*; Watts et al., "Health and Climate Change," 1861–1914.

disaster; others are psychosocial in nature, as when a drought-struck farming community is faced with the collapse of agriculture. All such effects share a common origin: a material blow administered by an unstoppable external force that consigns a person to emotional exile. This is *ecological grief*, a syndrome that first entered the discourse as *solastalgia*, "the distress produced by environmental change impacting on people while they are directly connected to their home environment."[92] When entire communities succumb, the psychopathology is both personal and social. Affected communities have been identified in the Australian Wheatbelt, among indigenous populations in Northern Canada, and in towns near open-cut coal-mining operations.

In ecological grief, the new "normal" begins upon realizing that the deterioration of one's home environment is irreversible and worsening. The *Umwelt* of everyday life, its material and emotional textures, have changed. One does not feel at-home while at home. *Home* has become a memory whose correlation with the real is ever diminishing. Victims of this syndrome are emotional refugees, resident aliens whose citizenship papers cannot be put in order.

Ecological grief is likely to affect large segments of the population after mid-century, once the fact of climate change is widely accepted and its personal consequences are widely felt. A grief-bound planet is a real-world possibility; its features can be imagined. Incrementally, then later in pulse-like surges, the shock of disbelief proceeds to uproar and outrage. Festivals meant to blunt fear and pacify the populace become bacchanalian routs. Flash meetings announced on what remains of bandwidth evolve into urban crime waves. Hopelessness and despair expand in widening swaths until they immobilize entire cities. Wandering pedestrians slump against downtown buildings, weeping in the streets. Fatigued bodies form milling crowds afloat on the moderating effect of narcotic and anti-depressant medications. Pharmaceutical companies earn fabulous

---

92. Albrecht et al., "Solastalgia," 95–98. For the psychopathology associated with climate change, see Clayton et al., *Mental Health*; Cunsolo and Landman, *Mourning Nature*. Some of the anxiety syndromes discussed in this literature are "screen" effects that function to dissipate and temporarily block anger, depression, and grief.

sums. Financial markets trade in rice, buffed and polished like Tiffany diamonds. Petty kings hoard food and water in security-encrusted compounds. Plebeians pound and rattle the gates until their rage gives way to the weakness of starvation. Dark horizons are etched with the spidery light of collapsing cell towers.[93]

The facts, figures, and projections reviewed in this chapter may appear dry and irrelevant until they are personalized, at which point their significance can be felt:

> My great-granddaughter will find the earth inhospitable and possibly deadly. Will she escape the routine risks of her struggling band—heat stress, nutritional deprivation, violence between neighboring factions? What spiritual tradition might this child learn were she to dodge the deadly sickle of the Anthropocene? Will she pour libations at the feet of leonine shamans carved in dark caverns? Will an old woman or man, an *Amma* or *Abba*, draw her attention to the fact that once upon a time, in another arid climate, in another time of upheaval, a certain God claimed absolute authority on the basis of infinite empathy?

A God whose self-transformation entailed the passage of death might have something personal and practical to say to followers who fear for their children's lives. Writers in the Orthodox tradition have addressed climate change; the Pope has issued an encyclical; Catholic and Protestant theologians have written technical articles.[94] Most of this work operates at high levels of abstraction,

---

93. This description is not wholly fantasy. It seems the super-rich in the tech and finance industries are planning for similar scenarios (Rushkoff, "Survival of the Richest").

94. For the Orthodox position, see Chryssavgis and Foltz, *Toward an Ecology of Transfiguration*. For the Roman Catholic position, see Pope Francis, *Encyclical Letter*. For a selection of theological articles, see Northcott and Scott, *Systematic Theology*. Process thinkers were early in discerning moral and theological aspects of environmental collapse (Cobb, *Is It Too Late?*). The situation is different among some fundamentalist Christian groups, whose views on climate change are bizarre from a scientific perspective (Sachdeva, "Religious

remote from concrete occasions of spiritual *praxis* and the data points of climate science. Will opportunities for the direct assimilation of Christian truths become fewer in number and reduced in quality as fanatic and conspiratorial voices rise to a deafening volume? Will doctrine and liturgy require a critical revision in order to serve the needs of persons born late this century when the material effects of climate change are more advanced and dire? Will ascetic and mystical theology assume critical importance when the rudiments of everyday life have become exceedingly harsh and the economic base and emotional utility of traditional religious institutions have deteriorated?

Identity," 1–36).

3

Empirical Apocalyptic

GLOBAL WARMING IS CHARACTERIZED in the first of the following essays as a process of scapegoating in which we, ourselves, perform as high priests of our own execution. The second essay examines the contemporary relevance of a passage in which the apostle Paul predicts an outbreak of "lawlessness" once a certain restraining force (*katechon*) is "taken from the scene" (2 Thess 2:1–12). The third and fourth essays track the moral roots of anthropogenic climate change: first, in the prehistory of the genus *Homo*; and, second, in empirical research that identifies a motivational factor that drives unethical ("sinful," "evil") behavior. The fifth and sixth essays address the eschatological significance of climate change. In the fifth, apocalyptic imagery in Jewish and Christian scripture is compared to the disaster scenarios studied in climate science. In the sixth, the theological concept of "end-time" is examined and adapted to the present historical moment. The contemporary relevance of another of Paul's descriptions of eschatological change is examined in the seventh essay (Rom 8:18–24). As he knew, so "we know that all creation groans and is in agony even until now" (8:22). A modern-day mystical vision that bears on the meaning of climate change is analyzed in the final essay.

GLOBAL SCAPEGOAT

Climate change initially and most harshly affects the poor, the marginalized, those without military hardware and surveillance capabilities. A statement endorsed by eighty-two medical societies outlines the risks:

> Climate change threatens everyone . . . , but is a more immediate danger to some. Climate change exacerbates health inequities, disproportionately harming the most vulnerable among us—children and pregnant women, people with low income, the aged and people with disabilities and chronic illnesses, some communities of color, indigenous people and tribal communities, immigrants, marginalized people of all races and ethnicities, and outdoor workers. Communities that have experienced systemic neglect and environmental racism have the least responsibility for climate pollution, but are the most affected.[1]

Similar points appear in publications concerned with human rights: "Perversely, while people in poverty are responsible for just a fraction of global emissions, they will bear the brunt of climate change, and have the least capacity to protect themselves. We risk a 'climate apartheid' scenario where the wealthy pay to escape overheating, hunger, and conflict while the rest of the world is left to suffer."[2]

The people at greatest risk rank no higher on the dominant scale of value than the resources beneath their feet. They are expendable, like stubble thrown on the fire. Their demise amounts to scapegoating on a global scale. The economic and demographic consequences of climate change surpass the scope of the colonial and imperialist projects. To the Greeks' *pharmakos*, to the errant goat of *Leviticus*, to the Aztecs' warrior captives, who were wined, dined, and sexually sated before their ritual murder—to these and countless other scapegoats we have added most of the human race.[3]

1. US. Call to Action, *On Climate, Health, and Equity*.

2. Alston, "UN Expert Condemns Failure."

3. For *pharmakos* (a human sacrificial victim), see Burkert, *Greek Religion*. For the biblical scapegoat, see Lev 16:22. For Aztec sacrifice of the captive

Certain biblical parables are relevant. The Good Samaritan is one, another is The Sheep and the Goats: "I assure you, as often as you neglected to do it to one of these least ones, you neglected to do it to me" (Mt 25:45).[4]

The "least ones" are mounting in number, like bonfires multiplying across the nighttime horizon. But something more than heaps of humans is at risk. The earth has joined the humans on a sacrificial altar of their own making. We have made ourselves the high priests of our own execution, the earth and its inhabitants serving as the altar and fuel of immolation.

Anthropogenic climate change is the consummation of the fundamental religious dynamic of sacrificial violence. No longer holy or hidden, its reign has become overt and secular. No longer selective in its targeting, its operatives and its victims are ubiquitous. No longer circumscribed in ecclesiastical calendars or periodic sacred rites, it is ongoing. Goya's painting *El Gigante* captures the immensity of the problem; the tiny figures fleeing along its lower edge capture our helplessness. The current scene of climate change can elicit a variety of emotional responses. At one extreme is anger, fury, and resentment; at the other is grief, sadness, and the vulnerability of melancholia. These states differ in value and represent varying stages of emotional adaptation to the threat of global warming. An unavoidable spiritual task during the early stages of adaptation is to know firsthand all these responses—otherwise one risks settling into preliminary states, locked in dead-end futility. Mere anger clouds moral judgement by amplifying its intensity and generalizing its application to absurd degrees. Resentment is scalding in its application, and personally corrosive. In comparison with these states, warranted

---

warrior, see Miller and Taube, *Illustrated Dictionary*. For scapegoating and climate change, see Northcott, "Girard, Climate Change, and Apocalypse," 287–310. For an economic perspective on climate change with a Girardian influence, see Dupuy, *Economy and the Future*.

4. This is the penultimate verse of the Olivet Discourse, which concludes: "They will go off to eternal punishment and the just to eternal life" (Mt 25:46). The "least ones" include especially children: "Children are the most vulnerable to the lifelong environmental effects caused by climate change arising . . . and from industry-linked pollution of the air, water, and land" (Clark et al., "A Future for the World's Children?," 609).

indignation is cognitively complex and genuinely eye-opening. Carefully wielded and intelligently honed, it is empowering and strategic in its targeting. In the case of global warming, it leads straightaway to moral condemnation. Hammer the gavel! Bring it down!

Informed moral reasoning is an important early step in forming an ascetic perspective that suits the emotional threats and moral darkness of the coming decades of the Anthropocene. In creating conceptual latticework that can hold steady against the flux of terrible change, it stabilizes emotion and settles the mind. Triple-checked moral judgements compensate for the revulsion of witnessing the failure of moral imagination that drives the human project of global warming. Inevitably, such judgements push back on the person who makes them, eliciting pain and penitence for personal acts of participation in the impassioned rush that is leading to our judgement. As such, moral reasoning is an ascetic practice for persons who wish to truly see the problem and discern the spiritual dimension of its catastrophic outcomes. The practice also produces mental outposts, the better to identify the "son of perdition," the responsible parties strolling in the halls of power and basking in showtime lights (2 Thess 2:3). Finally, informed moral reasoning inoculates against the passions, in this manner purifying attention and readying the practitioner for penitence and prayer. The practice has yet another benefit in promoting a cognitive perspective advised in eschatological texts:

> "Stay awake." (Mt 24:42)
> "Rouse yourself." (Rev 3:3)
> "You must be prepared." (Mt 24:44)
> "What I say to you, I say to all: Be on guard!" (Mk 13:37)
> "The moral is: Keep your eyes open." (Mt 25:13)

The scriptural context of each passage pairs terrible destruction and unpredictable, entirely spontaneous occasions of hopefulness and change. Only direct personal experience can resolve the paradox of anticipating certain destruction while expecting an entirely different outcome.[5]

---

5. Moltmann's remark is relevant: "Anyone who lives in necessary contradiction to the laws and powers of "this world" hopes for a new world of

"THE MYSTERY OF LAWLESSNESS"

Paul's second letter to the church at Thessalonica describes an unusual eschatological scenario that does not appear elsewhere in his writings (2 Thess 2:1–12).[6] The passage in question concerns an "adversary"—the "lawless one"—who disseminates "wicked deceit" and attempts to "seduce" its followers into "believing that the day of the Lord is here" (2 Thess 2:2, 3, 4, 8, 10). Presently, says Paul, a certain restraining force "holds him back," and will continue to do so until Christ returns and vanquishes the "workings of Satan" (2 Thess 2:7, 9). The contemporary relevance of this passage is the point of interest, specifically its bearing on the social and political upheavals that we can expect as the Anthropocene advances.[7]

The opening verses of the passage focus on the restraining force, whose exact nature is not made clear, as if Paul meant to allude and hedge rather than speak explicitly.[8] He does not say whether the restrainer (*katechon*) is a human agent, a body of law, or a supernatural entity that keeps in check "the secret force of lawlessness": "You know what restrains him until he shall be revealed in his own time. The mystery of lawlessness is already at work, mind you, but there is one who holds him back until that restrainer shall be taken from the scene" (2 Thess. 2:6–7). The passage continues as follows:

---

correspondences. The contradiction suffered is itself the negative mirror-image of the correspondence hoped for" (Moltmann, *Coming of God*). Simone Weil develops the same point in her dialectical philosophy (McCullough, *Religious Philosophy*).

6. For Paul's eschatology, see Blackwell et al., *Paul and the Apocalyptic Imagination*; Rowland, "Eschatology of the New Testament Church," 56–72. For early apocalyptic thought, see Daly, *Apocalyptic Thought*.

7. The passage (2 Thess. 2:1–12) has influenced modern political thought, most notably the work of Carl Schmitt (1888–1985), who saw it as the scriptural basis of a Christian conception of state power. More recently, and in a less secular vein, Giorgio Agamben has interpreted the removal of restraint as the doorway to messianic redemption, as reflected in the state's collapse and the Kingdom's arrival on earth (see Prozorov, "Katechon in the Age of Biopolitical Nihilism," 483–503).

8. Peerbolte, "κατέχον/κατέχων of 2 Thess. 2: 6–7," 138–50; Powell, "Identity of the 'Restrainer,'" 320–32.

> And then the lawless one will be revealed, whom the
> Lord will kill with the breath of his mouth and render
> powerless by the manifestation of his coming, the one
> whose coming springs from the power of Satan in every
> mighty deed and in signs and wonders that lie, and in
> every wicked deceit for those who are perishing because
> they have not accepted the love of truth so that they may
> be saved. Therefore, God is sending them a deceiving
> power so that they may believe the lie, that all who have
> not believed the truth but have approved wrongdoing
> may be condemned. (2 Thess. 2:8-12)

Paul wrote in broad strokes about an eruption of lawlessness preceding Christ's return. Beyond this understanding, the passage is obscure, indeed, "one of the most difficult in the New Testament."[9] A minority of scholars do not think Paul wrote this letter, and interpret "you know" ("You know what restrains him") as a rhetorical tactic, a way of harkening back to undisclosed or possibly nonexistent teachings of the historic Paul (2 Thess 2:6). In this manner, the author meant to draw the apostle's authority to his own non-Pauline epistle.

The mixed gender of the references complicates the meaning of *katechon*: the "what" that restrains is neuter—"you know what restrains him"—but the "one" who restrains is masculine—"there is one who holds him back" (2 Thess. 2:6, 7). Is the emperor Nero the restrainer, or perhaps the Roman Empire, which would administer law and enforce order during the time remaining before Christ's return? Or did Paul refer to the angels, who awaited their cue to intervene on earth in the final days. A clear (but simplistic) interpretation identifies Satan as "the lawless one" and God as the "restrainer" (2 Thess 2:7, 8).[10] Quite possibly, Paul viewed his own divinely appointed preaching mission as the restraining force that temporarily kept lawlessness in check. Once his mission was complete, restraint would give way and Christ would return.

The passage acquires new meaning now that the Anthropocene has begun and the prospects for advanced civilization are

9. Stephens, "Eschatological Themes."
10. Tonstad, "Restrainer Removed," 133–51.

diminishing. Once the passage's mythological content is bracketed, the restraining force that keeps lawlessness in check can be understood as a predictably modulated climate—the climate that has promoted the growth and orderliness of human culture since the advent of agrarian societies and that began eroding about two centuries ago.[11] Law and order, the orchestration of civic life, the distribution of power that ensured institutional continuity across political hierarchies and within sacred rites—all sought their mandates in Nature. The patterned regularity of a predictably modulated climate has been the real-world foundation of the growth and material success of civilization; and, for this same period of time, the climate held relatively constant. Those days have been "taken from the scene" now that the grindstone of deteriorative change is in motion: "There is no climate analog for this century at any time in at least the last 50 million years as measured by the annual emissions rate of carbon dioxide" (2 Thess 2:7).[12]

The passage can be drawn more closely into the present through selecting certain of Paul's words and assembling them in a narrative summary, while retaining the ambiguity that surrounds his portrayal of the power responsible for lawlessness:

> Now that a predictably modulated climate is being "taken from the scene," the "force of lawlessness" is becoming more powerful. Its effects are partly "revealed" and otherwise "secret," but its full force is "yet to come." Natural laws remain in force, but predicting their climatic effects is becoming increasingly difficult. Only raise the global average temperature another one or two degrees and the social and economic predations of global warming will become gross and obvious. Even now, "lawlessness" is "already at work" in "mighty deeds" of weather, in political "deceit," in pervasive and intrusive marketing, and, throughout the virtual world, in "signs and wonders that lie." Something personal seems to have taken charge— the "lawless one," who commands a "deceiving power"

---

11. For climate change in the early Holocene and its effects on agriculture and the development of civilization, see Fernandez-Armesto, "Farmers' Empire," 106–38; Jones, "Into a Warming World," 71–105.

12. Wuebbles et al., "Executive Summary."

that "springs from the power of Satan" and is a "manifestation of his coming." Its victims are easily tricked, their
gullibility turned against them. The "lawless one" baits
and leads them, and they come to "believe the lie." In this
sense, they are "perishing." For them, "lawlessness" is
cloaked in mystery—"the mystery of lawlessness," when,
in fact, the feeling of mysteriousness, of shrouded truths,
is a "wicked deceit," no more than a spell. Any mystery in
the advent of lawlessness is simply mystification, which
fascinates those attracted to "signs and wonders." The
feeling of shrouded truths, of the purported "power of
Satan," is nothing more than the advance of malevolence,
objective violence, and dissension for dissension's sake.
(2 Thess 2:3 et al.)

The *katechon* passage provides a general picture, as if Paul had
viewed the coming social and political crises of the Anthropocene
through binoculars with little magnification. Other scriptures of
eschatological import provide details, the Olivet Discourse in particular (Mt 24, 25; Mk 13; Lk 21). Throughout, the message is "wars
and rumors of wars," "wars and insurrections," "nation rising against
nation" (Mt 24:6,7; Lk 21:9). Predictably, much of this dissension
will entail state and corporate efforts to secure mineral resources,
arable land, and potable water. The West has enjoyed its "days of
Noah," its heyday of pleasure, leisure, and growth, of "eating and
drinking, marrying and giving in marriage," all the while remaining
"totally unconcerned" about the eventual consequences (Mt 24:37,
38, 39).[13] The developing nations have now joined the West, add-
ing to the earth's ever-increasing carbon burden.[14] The collective
guilt of the responsible parties—particularly in the power-house
developed nations—has become as intractable as forged steel.

My intention is not to play the fundamentalist and predict
the Antichrist's arrival. That would be paranoid fantasy, which
targets imaginary villains and assumes coherent plans where none

13. Noah's prophetic doom-saying has been discussed by Dupuy and Anders. Dupuy's starting point is climate change (Dupuy, "Precautionary Principle and Enlightened Doomsaying"). Anders's perspective is informed by the
invention of nuclear weapons (Dupuy, "Enlightened Doomsaying").

14. Friedlingstein et al., "Global Carbon Budget 2019," 1783–1838.

exists. *Satan* and *Antichrist* are monikers for chaos, deceit, and malevolence, much of it disguised in the "signs and wonders" flooding virtual space (2 Thess 2:9). The names do not imply a carefully orchestrated plan but, in fact, the opposite. One must not reason like Paul, but Paul's reasoning can be adapted to the social and political circumstances evolving during the Anthropocene. Rather than a coordinated design, something dumb and simple is at play: "mere anarchy is loosed," "the blood-dimmed tide is loosed," and any "ceremony of innocence" will be "drowned."[15] Yeats wrote "The Second Coming" in 1919, in the aftermath of World War I, in which 20 million people died. There have been many wars since then, and our power to inflict material damage and psychological havoc has grown exponentially.

FACE-TO-FACE AT NATARUK AND SIMA DE LOS HUESOS

Strife is certain to increase as climate change advances into the late twenty-first century. Military planners have recognized the risk and begun preparing for potential scenarios.[16] Revived nuclear threats and unguarded fissile material compound the threat of global warming. Tillich's expression "ultimate concern" has taken on a new and fearful meaning. What before was philosophical has become physical and crushingly real.

Cain has been killing Abel for at least ten thousand years, since the Nataruk rampage near Kenya's Lake Turkana, where one hunter-gatherer band murdered the members of another band.[17] This was a rich lacustrine environment at the time, not a landscape where scarcity might have precipitated the attack.[18] Group-inflicted

---

15. Yeats's poem can be found at the Poetry Foundation. https://www.poetry foundation.org/poems/43290/the-second-coming.

16. Brown and Crawford, *Rising Temperatures*; Rosenberg, "U.S. Navy Bracing for Climate Change"; Spratt and Dunlop, *Existential Climate-Related Security Risk*; Silliman, "Climate Change is a Threat."

17. Lahr et al., 'Inter-Group Violence," 394–98.

18. Lahr, "Discoveries at Nataruk."

mayhem among conspecifics did not appear *de novo* once modern humans developed. Chimpanzees mount bands of murderers.[19] The earliest murder yet discovered occurred 430,000 years ago, at the Sima de los Huesos site in Spain; both victim and perpetrator belonged to the Neandertal clade.[20]

There is no need to probe prehistory or track our animal ancestors to see how deeply ingrained is the human propensity for mayhem and murder. Only read the news. The most deadly mass murder in American history committed by a single individual occurred three days before I wrote this sentence.[21] The United States has the most mass murders per country.[22] Its suicide rate is rapidly increasing.[23] Its death rate has climbed each year since 2009, and its birth rate has fallen over four consecutive years, hitting a thirty-two-year low in 2018.[24] It is the scene of an escalating opioid epidemic.[25] Its annual rate of alcohol-related deaths more than doubled during the period from 1999 to 2017.[26] Most Americans are lonely; specifically, 61 percent of the adult population. A trend is apparent: the younger the age group, the lonelier, with loneliness intensifying in each group from 2018 to 2019.[27] While the country's level of carbon dioxide emissions ranks second to China's, its per capita emissions rate is nearly twice that of China.[28]

19. Pruetz et al., "Intragroup Lethal Aggression."

20. Sala et al., "Lethal Interpersonal Violence."

21. Fifty-eight persons were killed, 851 were injured (Wikipedia, "2017 Las Vegas Shooting").

22. Berkowitz et al., "Terrible Numbers."

23. The period of 1999 to 2016 saw 453,577 suicides, spread in roughly equal proportions across four age groups, ranging from 25 to 64 (Steelesmith et al., "Contextual Factors").

24. Hamilton et al., "Births: Provisional Data for 2018"; Macrotrends, "U.S. Death Rates 1950–2019."

25. For the period 1999 to 2018, nearly 450,000 people died from opioid overdose, and the number of deaths in 2018 was four times the number in 1999 (Center for Diseases Control and Prevention, "Opioid Overdose").

26. White et al., "Using Death Certificates."

27. Cigna, *Loneliness and the Workplace*, 8.

28. Union of Concerned Scientists, "Each Country's Share of CO2 Emissions."

To complete the picture, add military might and global financial domination. The combination of these statistics is a formula, not an accident. An interpretation could begin with addiction. There is not a better chemical agent than opioids to dull fear and blunt pain, to ease all discomfort while emptying the heart of authentic feeling and creating an illusory sensation of well-being. The addicts are functioning collectively like a cultural barometer. Apollonian and ageing, strutting and crippled, the United States is completing its teetering advance toward the extravaganza of complete cultural sterility, while fully armed and wagering on battle.

The discoveries at Nataruk and Sima de los Huesos are prehistoric probes of our fascination with mayhem and murder. The Spanish site may even reveal precursors of moral conscience. At Nataruk, none of the dead was buried, cannibalized, or subjected to ritual action. The bodies were discovered where they fell. Twelve victims were found intact. Fifteen or more additional bodies were not intact or have not been excavated. Six children were found nearby the adult female victims, this entire group resting apart from the males. Strikingly, "the remains of a 6- to 9-month-old fetus were recovered from within the abdominal cavity of one of the adult females."[29] The mother's hands and feet were bound despite her obviously gravid status. Defensive injuries (to the hand) were present in five bodies. Ten victims were struck on their heads, which showed penetrating injuries (from projectiles) in two cases and lethal blunt force trauma in seven. Of the victims showing blunt force trauma, all of the blows were to the front of the skull, shattering the frontal or temporal bones and in one case the mandible. The location of the traumatic blows bears special meaning in showing that the attackers and their victims could directly see one another. They were face-to-face and probably eye-to-eye.

The skull discovered at Sima de los Huesos is "the earliest evidence of lethal interpersonal violence in the hominin fossil record."[30] This young-adult male, identified as Cranium 17, died of lethal blunt-force trauma. His skull showed two perimortem

---

29. Lahr et al., "Inter-Group Violence," 395.
30. Sala et al., "Lethal Interpersonal Violence."

fractures of the frontal bone, "both caused by the same object . . . a tool of standardized size and shape": "The location of the lesions just to the left of the midline of the frontal squama . . . is consistent with the general pattern documented among recent humans, with most individuals showing lesions on the left side of the skull reflecting the predominance of right-handedness during face-to-face conflict."[31] A forensic examination led to the following conclusion:

> The type of injuries, their location, the strong similarity of the fractures in shape and size, and the different orientation and implied trajectories of the two fractures suggest they were produced by the same object in face-to-face interpersonal violence. Given that either of the two traumatic events was likely lethal, the presence of multiple blows implies an intention to kill.[32]

As with the bodies at Nataruk, the location of the blows shows that the attacker and the victim were face-to-face and probably eye-to-eye. The see-saw balance of the attacker's furor and the victim's terror was terminated by two rapidly executed, precisely placed blows, which erased their face-to-face encounter and rendered nil any prospect of its recurrence.

Something more than physical blows was in play at Nataruk and Sima de los Huesos. Recall that most of these murders occurred in the interpersonal setting of the face-to-face encounter, and that in most or all cases the attacker and the victim were eye-to-eye. The face of the person whose eyes meet mine is the embodied sign of a realization that inheres in most every social encounter: I am not the king, the dictator, the master of the moment, no matter my compulsion to adopt such roles. Rather, two of us are present—two of the same kind—and this is most obvious when we are face-to-face and eye-to-eye. I can deny this aspect of our meeting in favor of regal posing, in which case the ethical demand of our meeting is rejected. This demand is not an idea newly discovered on the occasion of each meeting. It precedes action, is anterior to thought, and bears

---

31. Sala et al., "Lethal Interpersonal Violence," 5, 7.
32. Sala et al., "Lethal Interpersonal Violence," 1.

high ethical significance. It is inchoate and pre-verbal when first present, like a bud awaiting the moment of flowering.

In the moment, the other's eyes have special significance. Their power of evocation and the opaque fullness of the pupils signal the observant presence of something inimitable that peers at me, awaiting my decision—a decision that favors either mercy or judgement. In the moment, will is decisive, as is the sympathetic reach of moral imagination. Shall I act or not? Is restraint and silence demanded, in which case my willfulness must be sacrificed? Shall I abdicate my self-appointed role as king and step forward as nakedly as the face that awaits my decision, or instead shall I press my claim and blot from my mind the ethical demand of the face-to-face encounter? In the latter case, I step into the road that leads ultimately to the impulse toward murder.

The preceding analysis appeals to Emmanuel Levinas, the Talmudic scholar and phenomenological philosopher who wrote at length on the face-to-face relation (*rapport de face à face*).[33] For Levinas, the face (*visage*) of the other person (*autrui*) differs from all other objects. Unlike objects that can be fixed in memory or photographs, examined clinically, or otherwise subjugated to my personal assumptions, the other's face renders futile all such efforts. Its expressive flux and flickering self-exposure are ever in retreat from my objectifying gaze and grasping intentions. The most vulnerable of personal displays, the other's face creates a precarious and easily endangered ethical relationship. It pleads with varying degrees of subtlety, awaiting my decision; and it opens, should I care to see, to an indefatigable Other.

A discursive exposition of the face-to-face encounter can proceed only so far. Twelve sentences from Levinas's writings will serve as a critical response to the murders at Nataruk and Sima de los Huesos. For that matter, they can serve as a critical response to all acts of murder and mayhem reaching back to Cain's:

1. The face of the Other . . . destroys and overflows the plastic image it leaves me, the idea existing to my own measure.[34]

33. Bergo, "Emmanuel Levinas"; Strasser, "Emmanuel Levinas," 612–52.

34. Levinas, *Totality and Infinity*, 50.

2. The face speaks to me and thereby invites me to a relation.[35]
3. The face resists possession, resists my powers.[36]
4. Access to the face is straightaway ethical.[37]
5. The face opens the primordial discourse whose first word is obligation.[38]
6. The gaze supplicates and demands . . . and is precisely the epiphany of the face as a face.[39]
7. The skin of the face is that which stays naked, most destitute. . . . There is an essential poverty in the face; the proof of this is that one tries to mask this poverty by putting on poses, by taking on a countenance. The face is exposed, menaced, as if inviting us to an act of violence. At the same time, the face is what forbids us to kill.[40]
8. The Other manifests itself by the absolute resistance of its defenseless eyes. . . . The infinite in the face (brings) into question my freedom, which is discovered to be murderous and usurpatory.[41]
9. The first word of the face is the "Thou shalt not kill." It is an order. There is a commandment in the appearance of the face, as if a master spoke to me.[42]
10. An infinite resistance to murder . . . gleams in the face of the Other, in the total nudity of his defenseless eyes, in the nudity of the absolute openness of the Transcendent.[43]
11. The being that presents himself in the face comes from a dimension of height, a dimension of transcendence where he

---

35. Levinas, *Totality and Infinity*, 198.

36. Levinas, *Totality and Infinity*, 197.

37. Levinas, *Difficult Freedom*, 85.

38. Levinas, *Difficult Freedom*, 201.

39. Levinas, *Difficult Freedom*, 75.

40. Levinas, *Ethics and Infinity*, 85, 86.

41. Levinas, *Difficult Freedom*, 296.

42. Levinas, *Ethics and Infinity*, 89.

43. Levinas, *Ethics and Infinity*, 199.

can present himself as a stranger without opposing me as ob-
stacle or enemy.[44]

12. In the face the Other expresses his imminence, the dimension
of height and divinity from which he descends.[45]

Certain words in these sentences can be gathered and reassembled
to create a narrative summary:

> The "demands" of the face-to-face relationship become
> apparent when "posing" has ceased, when the busy effort
> of "taking on a countenance" has stopped. The other's
> face is then seen differently, as "naked," "exposed," "des-
> titute," as "menaced" and "defenseless." An "essential
> poverty" is apparent, and yet the "defenseless eyes" pose
> an "absolute resistance." The other's face "invites me to a
> relation" and expressly "forbids us to kill." It "resists my
> powers" and desire for "possession," and so tests my urge
> toward "an act of violence." It is epiphanic in its "dimen-
> sion of height and divinity," in revealing "the absolute
> openness of the Transcendent." It "invites" the "Other"
> to "present himself as a stranger without opposing me
> as an obstacle or enemy." This invitation "to a relation"
> can be found intolerable. Why? Because the "infinite in
> the face" puts in "question my freedom," my "murderous
> and usurpatory" freedom. The most benighted response
> to this perceived threat is "murder."[46]

The victim at Simos de los Huesos was discovered at the bottom of a vertical shaft, a natural chimney thirteen meters in depth.
At least twenty-eight additional bodies have been found within this
bone dump. Presumably, the man identified as Cranium 17 was
thrown or pushed down the shaft by the person who killed him. Is it
correct to say he was *buried*, which implies self-reflection and a ritual aspect in depositing the corpse?[47] Or was his body dumped with

44. Levinas, *Ethics and Infinity*, 215.

45. Levinas, *Totality and Infinity*, 262.

46. Levinas, *Ethics and Infinity*, 85, 86, 199, 215; Levinas, *Difficult Freedom*,
75, 296; Levinas, *Totality and Infinity*, 50, 198, 197, 262.

47. For Neanderthal burials in the period c 200,000 to c 12,000 BP, see
Fernandez-Armesto, "Mind in the Ice," 42–70.

the intent of hiding it as quickly and secretly as possible? I suppose an inarticulate persecutory whisper echoed around the murderer, as with Cain: "What have you done! Listen: your brother's blood cries out to me from the soil!" (Gen 4:10). I suppose this whisper of conscience compelled the action of dumping the body as quickly as possible, so as to quieten its echo.

THE DARK CORE OF PERSONALITY

The two preceding analyses trace the roots of murder, mayhem, lawlessness, and deceit: first, in a Pauline epistle, and second in the prehistory of the genus *Homo*. The quest continues with a re-evaluation of the doctrine of original sin. The purpose throughout is to ascertain the inception point of the human project of destroying the habitability of the planet, in this manner bringing countless species, possibly including ourselves, to grief or death.

Original sin has always been conceived as an ingrained constant throughout humankind, but little else about the doctrine has met with ongoing consensual agreement. Is original sin an irrational motivation and specifically the source of concupiscence? Is it a certain willfulness whose outcome is blasphemy or idolatry? Is it a social propensity that inevitably incites strife, or a spiritual discomposure that clouds moral focus? An ascetic might say that *original sin* is a technical term for the passions, which drive craving and remain insurmountable apart from ascetic practice. In the Christian Neoplatonist perspective advocated by Augustine, original sin is the outcome of an absence of being, this absence functioning in the moral sphere as the gravitational force of dark matter functions in the physical cosmos. Dark matter arranges and distorts the space and material around it; so original sin bends and twists human intentions. The meaning of original sin can also be pursued in scientific terms: if original sin is not propagated through supernatural means or strictly through social learning, is it a heritable disposition whose material basis is the mechanisms of behavioral genetics?[48] Whatever the case, the doctrine holds that this sinful constant is universally present.

48. Cf. Peterson, "Falling Up," 273–86.

"Original" connotes fixed, settled, old, like a benchmark indicating a remote starting point. In this sense, original sin refers to a source that has given rise to a lineage. Substituting "originative" for "original" adds a measure of clarity. Thus, originative sin suggests a simmering, generative, infiltrative harmfulness, analogous to a pediatric head injury whose pathological consequences become more obvious as development occurs.

A certain psychological interpretation of original sin proves meaningful, the more so because it derives from large-group studies that rest on decades of prior research.[49] On this basis, original sin can be understood as the inception point of nine injurious, ethically flawed personality traits. These traits devolve from a single source called the *dark core of personality*, which is defined as "the general tendency to maximize one's individual utility—disregarding, accepting, or malevolently provoking disutility for others—, accompanied by beliefs that serve as justification."[50] The appeal to utilitarian ethical theory in this definition is not particularly helpful. The dark core, once it imposes itself in given cases, has an agential and cognitive quality and is intimately linked with emotion (or, in some cases, the abnormal absence of emotion). Its operation is more like a state of possession than a moral calculus.

Trait indicates chronicity or redundancy over time. Its use in personality science implies that the dark core is biologically rooted in either its origin or the power of its manifestation. Dark traits are variously elicited, shaped, and suppressed through social learning, but something autonomous and generative is also in question. This something is the dark core of personality; the inception point of nine personality traits and the reference point when speaking of original sin.[51]

49. Moshagen et al., "Dark Core of Personality," 656–88. The quotations in the main text are from the in-press version of this article.

50. Moshagen et al., "Dark Core of Personality" (in press), 87. The paired dash and comma appear in the original publication.

51. Societal and psychological barriers that limit mitigation and adaptation to climate change are addressed in Adger et al., "Are There Social Limits," 290–302.

Four traits (the so-called "dark tetrad") were well-known before the dark core of personality was identified:

1. Psychopathy ("lack of empathy");[52]
2. Narcissism ("excessive self-absorption");[53]
3. Machiavellianism ("the belief that ends justify the means");[54]
4. Sadism ("a longstanding pattern of cruel or demeaning behavior toward others," with the goal of "asserting power and dominance or for pleasure and enjoyment").[55]

The remaining traits include:

5. Egoism ("excessive concern with one's own pleasure or advantage at the expense of community wellbeing");[56]
6. Moral Disengagement (a "cognitive orientation" that promotes unethical behavior "without feeling distress");[57]
7. Psychological Entitlement ("a stable and pervasive sense that one deserves more and is entitled to more than others");[58]
8. Self-interest ("the pursuit of gains in socially valued domains," such as "money or social status");[59]
9. Spitefulness ("readiness to inflict harm on another person even when it entails harm to oneself").[60]

The traits are closely linked; some are reciprocally related. They are not added or summed to create the dark core, like the pieces of a puzzle or the ingredients of a recipe. The dark core of personality is their common origin and, in the statistical sense, the source of their shared variance.

52. Moshagen et al., "Dark Core of Personality" (in press), 87.
53. Moshagen et al., "Dark Core of Personality" (in press), 87.
54. Moshagen et al., "Dark Core of Personality" (in press), 87.
55. Moshagen et al., "Dark Core of Personality" (in press), 87.
56. Moshagen et al., "Dark Core of Personality" (in press), 87.
57. Moshagen et al., "Dark Core of Personality" (in press), 87.
58. Moshagen et al., "Dark Core of Personality" (in press), 87.
59. Moshagen et al., "Dark Core of Personality" (in press), 87.
60. Moshagen et al., "Dark Core of Personality" (in press), 87.

To this point, two frames of reference have been in play. One is psychological and focused on a malevolent personality factor; the other is doctrinal and focused on the concept of original sin. A third frame of reference can be added—the mythological, with Satan admitted as an imaginal embodiment of original sin and the dark core of personality. These tightly meshed frames of reference span the psyche, religious anthropology, and the imaginal world of dreaming and world mythology. Satan personifies a point of doctrine and is the mythological transformation of a concept of religious anthropology. As the dark core is a single unified factor, so Satan is an independent agent rather than an aggregate of errant supernatural tendencies. He may call himself "legion" when speaking as the Gerasene, but he did so with a single voice (Mk 5:9). As the dark core disseminates the effects of nine traits, so Satan's power fractionates, dispersing into the forms of many demons. Satan (the proper noun) indicates particularly malevolent expressions of sinfulness; and in the psychological frame of reference, refers to highly malicious configurations of moral action channeled outward from the dark core of personality. Evil is in question.

Dark traits are obvious in many leaders past and present, and the same traits inflame their followers. Their opponents become similarly provoked, at which point the respective motivational states of leaders, followers, and opponents are identical despite obvious differences in their stated beliefs. Strife, dissension, and hatred follow when the dark core manifests as such. Virtual communication intensifies these contagious circumstances much like the Third Reich's ambitious public address system at the Nuremberg Rallies, where the predatory message of flesh-eating Dionysius was circumambient and unavoidable.[61] The same message is broadcast today and will increase in volume and multiply across media and platforms as the socioeconomic pressures imposed by climate change erode the fabric of civil society. Power has changed hands. It barely scratches the surface to say that the cultural forces driving the Anthropocene are charged with hubris. Prometheus, Faust, and all the soaring flights based on new technology are flyweight

---

61. Dionysios Omestes, the "eater of raw flesh," was a hunter and beast of prey (Otto, *Dionysus*, 109).

fantasies compared to the throne that governs our time. A closer approximation is Milton's gloating prince: "Better to reign in Hell, than serve in Heav'n."[62] A certain force has taken charge—slit-eyed, shiny, equally galvanic and insidious. Sheltering in masks, he directs from the wings, executing the superb stagecraft of his melodramas of hatred. Engaged in noisy rites, he is Bromios—the Roarer, the Loud Shouter.[63] Overt signs of his presence include concussive bellowing, thudding weaponry, and blood-lust shouting in sporting arenas. But he moves as easily in pure specimens of stealth, disguised in immersive marketing and peering from the dull eyes and lulled minds of his tech-addicted minions.[64] Stripped of his impressive leopard skin, he takes to the air, rising in spumes of emotion and infusing his followers with animosity and panic. His incense is the poisonous incantations of large social gatherings. His aphrodisiac is mass psychology. Seeded in gullible mobs, he dances in frissons of hatred and trades in clichés of resentment. His intoxicated followers move in lock-step with his high-stepping gait and finger-pointing antics before succumbing to the passivity of his drugged and virtual fantasies—mimics one and all, preening in clapped-out routines and priding themselves on secrets. But most cool, and malicious as a lacerating blade, is the pleasure he takes in financial reports that are witting affronts to those who are personally harmed.

Can the dark core be held in check as climate change advances, as our fragile organizational structures succumb, as the echo chamber of digital communication amplifies fear and hatred? On the scale of large social collectives—no. Among the spiritually avid and their remnant bands—yes. "I saw Satan fall like lightning" (Lk 10:18).[65]

62. Milton, *Paradise Lost*, I:263.

63. In the earliest references, the god Dionysus is called Bromios (the "Roarer," the "Loud Shouter") in his role as the leader of "noisy rites" (Lang, *Homeric Hymns*, 217).

64. For tech-addiction, see Weinstein and Lejoyeux, "New Developments," 117–25; Zhu et al., "Molecular and Functional Imaging." For the personal and social pathology associated with social media and internet use, see Kramer et al., "Experimental Evidence," 8788–90; Lancaster, "You Are the Product," 3–10; Shakya and Christakis, "Association of Facebook Use," 203–11.

65. Lk. 10:18 is regarded as an authentic saying of the historical Jesus

ESCHATOLOGY IN THE ANTHROPOCENE

Eschatology (from *eschatos*, meaning "final," "farthest," "utmost") is the theological project of systematic reflection on the "last things."[66] These "things" vary considerably in content and respective levels of abstraction, but all concern events set to occur toward the end of time, when history is brought to a conclusion. The traditional topics of eschatology include: afterlife and the fate of the soul; the general resurrection, when all rise; heaven and hell, and the judgment that destines a person for one or the other; and Christ's *parousia*, His "coming presence in glory."[67] Another concern lingers behind the others but is rarely addressed systematically in scripture: theodicy, the theological project of vindicating God's goodness in a world rife with evil.[68] Yet another area of content is basic to traditional eschatology and of special interest at present. This is Apocalyptic, understood as a scriptural genre whose most prolific period of development began in the third century BCE and tapered off during the first two centuries CE. All Christian apocalyptic writings are outgrowths of Jewish scripture and reflection. *Revelation* is a leading example.[69]

(Gathercole, "Jesus' Eschatological Vision," 143–63). This verse is likely a personal report of a mystical vision. Certain features suggest as much: its concision, declarative tone, and emotional forcefulness; its discontinuity with surrounding text; and its mythological semantic and visual content. The verse portrays a process of reversal in which the "fall" or downward transformation of Satan (evil, injustice, subversion of the Father) is paired with Jesus's rise to power and the success of his appointed missionaries, the "seventy-two" (Lk 10:1). Such reversals (in emotion, mental content, or dominant perceptual modality) occur regularly in the processes that mediate mystical experience based on the principle of *mystical enantiodromia* (Bradford, "Emotion in Mystical Experience," 103–18; Bradford, *Spiritual Tradition*).

66. For a current and comprehensive resource, which includes non-Christian traditions, see Walls, *Oxford Handbook of Eschatology*.

67. Moltmann, *Coming of God*, 25. "To translate *parousia* as 'coming again' or 'second coming' is wrong, because that presupposes a temporary absence" (25–26).

68. Peterson, "Eschatology and Theodicy," 518–34.

69. Collins outlines the historical precedents of Jewish and Christian apocalyptic scripture: "It is generally agreed that apocalyptic writings draw on ancient

Apocalyptic is loyal to a historical perspective but time-bending in its manner of reporting past events. The narrative technique of *ex eventu* prophecy ("prediction after the outcome") allows its authors to speak in the voice of past historical or fictive figures who predict certain political and religious crises that actually occurred, or are imagined to have occurred, before the authors' and readers' own lifetimes.[70] Peering backward along a linearly arranged historical sequence, readers witness the unfolding of crises that model or serve as precedents for a present crisis. That an earlier crisis was foretold is evidence of God's plan at work in history. Apocalyptic is meant to inspire hope amid crisis. Its use of code (coded names, dates, locations, and figures both real and imagined) reflects the danger faced by the religious minority to whom the scripture is addressed. In its intent and for its targeted audience, Apocalyptic is not otherworldly:

> Revelation was not written for "rapturists" fleeing from the world, who tell the world "goodbye" and want to go to heaven; it was meant for resistance fighters, struggling against the godless powers on this earth, especially the nuclear powers; it was written, that is, out of love for this world of God's.[71]

Apocalyptic might be characterized as prophetically inspired *samizdat*.

Apocalyptic scripture is highly imaginative and somewhat predictable in narrative structure. Its supernatural interventions

---

Near Eastern myths, and various aspects of apocalypticism are paralleled in Greco-Roman tradition. Prophetic material that is somewhat analogous to the Jewish apocalypses can be found in Egyptian tradition in the Hellenistic period. None of these traditions . . . offer such comprehensive analogies as the Persian material, although they may have influenced individual Jewish texts at various points. . . . It would be far too simple, however, to say that the whole phenomenon of apocalypticism was imported to Judea from Persia. It also had roots in Jewish tradition (Collins, "Apocalyptic Eschatology," 42, 43).

70. For *ex eventu* prophecy (*vaticinium ex eventu*), see Collins, "Apocalyptic Eschatology," 42.

71. Moltmann, *Coming of God*, 153. The phrase "nuclear powers" is probably a double entendre. Moltmann likely meant to encourage readers to engage in resistance to nuclear proliferation.

and cast of characters reflect mythological thinking. Among its concerns are the divine and angelic interventions that will vanquish the forces of evil, bring our present world to an end, and usher in "a new heaven and a new earth" (Rev 21:1; Is 65:17). All manner of tectonic and celestial upheavals coincide with the shutting down of history. Some can be described as natural disasters, others involve warfare. Skies darken, earthquakes erupt, lightning flashes, and "giant hailstones like huge weights come crashing down" (Rev 16:21). Rivers, springs, and oceans are suddenly polluted, and all the creatures therein die. The idolatry and moral corruption that have poisoned political institutions and human interaction are judged and punished. Mighty kingdoms fall. Disastrous events of a sociopolitical nature run parallel with equally dramatic disturbances to the natural order.

Apocalyptic texts pulse with ill will and prophetic ire. Righteous judicial emotion is attributed to the angels and the Savior, and such emotion is displayed in graphic terms in acts of judgment and retribution. Angels abound in these texts; some are good soldiers, others, minions of evil. They can be as huge as titans as they stride across the earth, brandishing weaponry of fire and destruction. The droughts and warming caused by climate change have contributed to wildfires and "scorched land" on every continent the past few years (Rev 8:7). Even permafrost and taiga are burning, releasing long-dormant pathogens, naturally occurring mercury (a potent neurotoxin), and methane ("a greenhouse gas that is around 30 times more potent than CO_2").[72] Wildfires might be imagined as avenging angels descending on the perpetrators of global warming. That they harm innocent persons far removed from the halls of power accords with the notion of collective guilt and the attribution of blame in social environments shaped by mass psychology.

The ancient writers' cosmology is very different from our own, which makes the comparison of apocalyptic disasters and the disasters induced by global warming a delicate matter. They assumed

72. Lenton et al., "Climate Tipping Points," 594. For the release of methane and mercury, see Richter-Menge et al., *2019: Arctic Report Card 2019;* Heilig, "Greenhouse Gas Methane (CH4)," 109–37. For methane release in petroleum mining, see Alvarez et al., "Assessment of Methane Emissions," 186–88.

that the entire cosmos would be subject to apocalyptic change. We know that global warming affects only the speck called planet Earth. It is anthropocentric and common to believe the earth matters on the large stage of the physical cosmos; but it is also reasonable for theists to suppose that something about human mentation makes it special or uniquely prized by the Creator. By no means is the instrumental intelligence of *homo faber* in question. The *telos* of his wizardry is global warming, mass extinction, and self-destruction. Ever-restless *homo faber*, chained in a court of his own making, awaits his judge in the form of global warming.

Reports of melting ice, unprecedented heat waves, and other climatic aberrations of the Anthropocene make daily appearances in the popular press. The newsworthiness of these reports rapidly peaks and fades, as if there could be a bigger story. Apocalyptic imagery has become topical—the weather report has accrued religious significance. Certain analogies are apparent:

a. The upheavals in the natural order portrayed in apocalyptic scripture are analogous to the disaster scenarios studied in the science of global warming.

b. The plot lines of apocalyptic scripture are determined by eschatological beliefs. The climate-related disasters studied by scientists are framed in numbers, formulas, and predictive models. The eschatological plotting that informs apocalyptic scripture is analogous to the numeracy, research designs, and statistical procedures that serve climate science.

c. As apocalyptic scripture describes tumultuous natural events that encompass the entire cosmos and signal the end of history, so the science of global warming investigates worldwide climatic changes that will cause mass extinction, contribute to the erosion of high civilization, and possibly render much of the earth uninhabitable.

d. As the end-time events of apocalyptic scripture are provoked by moral corruption and blasphemy and the injustice of human institutions, so the natural disasters studied in the science of global warming are anthropogenic in origin. Of the anthropogenic factors, some draw form and motivational power from the dark core of personality. In this sense and to this degree, the inception point of global warming is original sin.

e. To condense and encapsulate this line of thought: the science of global warming is real-world apocalyptic.

Gunther Anders comments on this very kind of reversal, in which mythological content shifts ontological register and becomes empirical. He writes: "We are not speaking metaphorically when we name what is in front of us 'apocalyptic.' In light of our situation, the way people spoke of the 'end' back then (in 'Apostolic Christianity') was metaphoric."[73]

Natural disasters are becoming increasingly unnatural as we embed ourselves more deeply in the natural order. Global warming is provoking the occurrence of such disasters, amplifying their intensity, and in some instances functioning as their *sine quo non*. Consider the wildfires currently ravaging Australia. The years of draught and record-high temperatures induced by global warming primed their occurrence and are promoting their growth.[74] Natural disasters in which human endeavor plays a major role can be gathered in a new category of religious phenomena—that of *empirical apocalyptic*. Two kinds of disasters are included: those in which global warming is a remote material cause, like the wildfires in Australia; and those in which human intervention plays a direct, decisive, and specific causal role, like the environmental consequences of the 2010 Deepwater Horizon oil spill, the largest marine spill in American history. Empirical apocalyptic and traditional Apocalyptic are distinct but overlapping categories. Their major difference is obvious: empirical apocalyptic concerns real-world events of a physical nature, whereas the disasters described in apocalyptic scripture are the purported material consequences of supernatural intervention, like the oceanic dead zones caused by the trumpet blast of an avenging angel (Rev 8:9, 16:3). The disasters of empirical apocalyptic are reported as facts, formulas, and predictive models in the scientific literature. Stringent criteria determine

---

73. Anders, "Apocalypse without Kingdom," 7. The parenthetical insertion is mine, but the phrase "Apostolic Christianity" is Anders's.

74. Freedman, "'Megafire.'"

what data are permitted and their manner of presentation. Traditional Apocalyptic draws on preexisting scripture in responding to regional political crises and is further constrained by religious beliefs and sanctioned doctrine. Its literary medium is rich in metaphor and symbols and allows for coded messages that address oppressed religious minorities. The two forms of apocalyptic appeal to different lexicons, styles, epistemologies, mindsets—they appeal to different "worlds" and reflect different ontological premises. And yet they overlap and all but merge within a band of mutual resemblance. The zone of overlap is determined on moral grounds: all the phenomena within this band evolve across their respective chains of causation from a common core—the dark core of personality. In other words, all the wreckage—real or imagined—is a reckoning with the activated force of original sin. A certain scripture, which might otherwise be read as a religious cliché, is newly relevant once its body of references is broadened to include the effects of global warming: "The wages of sin is death," where "death" means barren, polluted, infertile, arid, flooded, or blazing (Rom 6:23).

Were neighboring tectonic plates to shift and cause an earthquake that destroys San Francisco, the earthquake and consequent damages would *not* be examples of empirical apocalyptic. Global warming is not unsettling the Pacific and the North American plates. The Deepwater Horizon spill and the earthquakes caused by hydraulic fracking are a different matter.[75] Both exemplify empirical apocalyptic, and both concern petroleum mining. Their correlates in traditional Apocalyptic are the earthquakes, fires, and marine pollution that strike the earth on "the great day of the Lord" (Zeph 1:14). As the disastrous events of traditional Apocalyptic are provoked by moral corruption and the injustice of governing bodies, so the spill and the earthquakes are material symbols of the dark core working in the executives, the board members, and the political supporters of the responsible corporate entities. To varying degrees, those who crave and buy these companies' products bear culpability as well. The dark traits on display in the two examples—including the

75. Rubenstein, "Induced Earthquakes"; Witman, "More Earthquakes." The underground disposal of wastewater is apparently responsible for fracking-related earthquakes.

obfuscation, evasion, and legal tactics of the responsible parties—encompass Moral Disengagement, Machiavellianism, Self-Interest, and Psychological Entitlement.[76] In cases of extreme suffering and exorbitant cost, the traits of Psychopathy and Sadism are active as well. These traits have been granted full license under the shield of the neoliberal economy and form a psychological web that binds the world in avarice. Gathering *en masse* behind this shield, humans behave like top predators, forming improvised packs and turning on one another after killing their initial prey.

The Deepwater Horizon spill bears clear apocalyptic resonance. Recall the news reports of "flames cast into the sea," the pollution of "rivers and springs," and the dead zones where "every living thing in the sea died" (Rev 8:8, 10, 11; 16:3). Fracking-related earthquakes mimic a form of disturbance that coincides with critical eschatological junctures. An earthquake occurred at the moment of Jesus's death (Mt 27:52), and another when his disappearance from the tomb was first announced (Mt 28:2). Another struck when the apostle Paul was imprisoned: "A severe earthquake suddenly shook the place, rocking the prison to its foundations. Immediately all the doors flew open and everyone's chains were pulled loose" (Acts 16:26). The earth responded while "Paul and Silas were praying," releasing them to continue their preaching mission (Acts 16:25). Yet another earthquake signals the start of the final reckoning, "the great day of vengeance":

> When I saw the Lamb break open the sixth seal, there
> was a violent earthquake; the sun turned black as a goat's
> hair tentcloth and the moon grew red as blood. The stars
> in the sky fell crashing to earth like figs shaken loose by
> a mighty wind. Then the sky disappeared as if it were a
> scroll being rolled up; every mountain and island was
> uprooted from its base. The kings of the earth, the nobles
> and those in command, the wealthy and the powerful,
> the slave and the free—all hid themselves in caves and
> mountain crags. They cried out to the mountains and
> rocks, "Fall on us! Hide us from the face of the One who

76. These dark traits are discussed in an earlier essay: "The Dark Core of Personality."

sits on the throne and from the wrath of the Lamb! The great day of vengeance has come. Who can withstand it?" (Rev 6:12–17)

According to a common exegetical perspective, the aberrant natural phenomena described in traditional apocalyptic texts reflect a rhetorical strategy whose effectiveness is based on the pre-scientific mindset and magical thinking of the texts' authors and original audience. In ancient times, spiritual effects were thought to ricochet throughout the natural order, instigating material change on a supernatural basis. The authors tagged these effects with presumptive natural phenomena, like the earthquake that coincided with Jesus's death. Granted this perspective, the apocalyptic scenarios must be demythologized, the better to discern their existential meaning.[77] Their eccentric content, in deviating from the natural order (as we understand it), is like a flare signaling events of great religious importance. The true, present-day meaning of these events becomes clear only after the aberrant content has been bracketed. The purged text, free of supernatural effects, is the true text.

This perspective is losing persuasiveness as we pass more deeply into the Anthropocene. All manner of anthropogenic disturbances within the natural order are material evidence of an apocalyptic era of our own making. These disturbances are evidence of spiritual nescience and, in the case of the mining examples, resource depletion at the cost of environmental collapse. They display original sin in active mode, understood as the dark

77. I refer to Bultmann's program of demythologization and existential hermeneutics (Bultmann, *New Testament*). Consider Moltmann's response to Bultmann's program as applied to New Testament eschatology: "Rudolph Bultmann still believed in 1941 that 'mythical eschatology is untenable for the simple reason that the parousia of Christ never took place as the New Testament expected. History did not come to an end, and, as every sane person knows, it will continue to run its course.' Today the notion that world history will continue to run its course is nothing more than wishful thinking. 'Every sane person' is aware of the nuclear, ecological and economic catastrophes that threaten the modern world. The apocalyptic eschatology which Bultmann considered 'mythical' is more realistic than his faith in the inexorable onward course of world history" (Moltmann, *Coming of God*, 135).

core of personality working in the responsible parties. Adverse spiritual effects *are* ricocheting throughout the natural order; the Anthropocene is the unrivalled example.

END-TIMES

James Watt's improved steam engine was released commercially in 1776, marking the beginning of a transitional period that we have brought to an end. Power has changed hands, the scepter having passed from God the Creator to the most clever and dangerous of His creatures. What before was *creatio ex nihilo*—a donation of global proportions—is now *reductio ad nihil*—our destruction of a habitable planet.[78] In pairing the Latin phrases, I follow the theologian Ulrich Körtner, who drew on the critic Gunther Anders.[79] Anders's main theme is the West's Promethianism, its project of reducing living matter, ourselves included, to machines.[80] Anders died in 1992, too soon to follow the Promethean project toward its consummation in digital technology, robotics, artificial intelligence, and the utopian fantasies of the Transhumanist movement. In Anders's usage, *reductio ad nihil* refers to the invention of nuclear weapons and our power to terminate life on earth through warfare. Similarly, Körtner had in mind the atomic bomb when he wrote: "The Lutheran conception of an eschatology of *annihilatio mundi*, a conception largely rejected during the subsequent history of theology, has in an utterly unexpected fashion become a real possibility as a result of the nuclear threat."[81] The eschatology of *annihilatio mundi* holds that the world will be burned to nothingness, leaving only the angels, the faithful, and God.[82] The Reformed tradition

78. The *creatio ex nihilo* ("creation from nothing") formulation was developed in the second century by the apologists Clement, Tertullian, and Theophilus in their effort to combat gnostic metaphysics and to "ensure the sovereignty and freedom of God" (Pelikan, *Christian Tradition*, 36).

79. Körtner, *End of the World*.

80. Little of Anders's work has been translated in English; see, for example, Müller, *Promethianism*.

81. Körtner, *End of the World*, 181.

82. Pinnock, "Annihilationism," 462–75.

opposed this line of thought, preferring *transformatio mundi* to *annihilatio mundi*. As a point of contrast, both positions can be set against the Orthodox teaching of *glorificatio mundi*.[83]

Jürgen Moltmann, who is largely responsible for reviving the field of eschatology in the late twentieth century, opposed the doctrine of *annihilatio mundi*.[84] Speaking in 1993, he said:

> I think annihilation is unthinkable. . . . What is cannot become nothing again . . . . So, the idea of annihilation is, I think, an impossible idea. You may believe in annihilation but you can never combine this with faith in God the Creator. That God the Creator will, at the end, annihilate everything that he created and annihilate things for which his own Son died? I think it is impossible. That at the end there is a big "No"?[85]

Forces other than God the Creator have assumed control since 1993, and their power has become inestimable. In 2018, climate scientists studying the future trajectories of the Earth System proposed a planetary *telos* that resembles the eschatological outcome described in theologies of annihilation:

> We explore the risk that self-reinforcing feedbacks could push the Earth System toward a planetary threshold that, if crossed, could prevent stabilization of the climate at intermediate temperature rises and cause continued warming on a "Hothouse Earth" pathway even as human emissions are reduced. Crossing the threshold would lead to a much higher global temperature than any interglacial period in the past 1.2 million years and to sea levels significantly higher than at any time in the Holocene.[86]

In saying "stabilization of the climate at intermediate temperature rises," the authors refer to "~2°C above the preindustrial level."[87]

83. Louth, "Eastern Orthodox Eschatology," 233–47.

84. Moltmann, *Coming of God*, 267–69.

85. Moltmann, "Talk-Back Session," 41, 42.

86. Steffen et al., "Trajectories of the Earth System," 8252.

87. Steffen et al., "Trajectories of the Earth System," 8252, 8254.

That we will reach or exceed this level within the present century is not an uncommon or extreme opinion.[88]

Granted the Hothouse Earth trajectory is avoided, there remains the present certainty that warming is progressing faster than previously thought:

> In October (2018), the Intergovernmental Panel on Climate Change (IPCC) released a report setting out why we must stop global warming at 1.5°C above preindustrial levels . . . . If the planet warms by 2°C—the widely touted temperature limit in the 2015 Paris climate agreement—twice as many people will face water scarcity than if warming is limited to 1.5°C. That extra warming (of 0.5°C) will also expose more than 1.5 billion people to deadly heat extremes, and hundreds of millions of individuals to vector-borne diseases such as malaria, among other harms. But the latest IPCC special report underplays another alarming fact: global warming is accelerating. Three trends—rising emissions, declining air pollution, and natural climate cycles—will combine over the next twenty years to make climate change faster and more furious than anticipated.[89]

The authors anticipate our crossing the 1.5°C threshold by 2030, and the 2°C limit by 2045.

The scientists who emphasize the importance of our stabilizing "the climate at intermediate temperature rises" have recommended a plan of collective action that could compensate for the identified risks:[90]

> Collective human action is required to steer the Earth System away from a potential threshold and stabilize it in a habitable interglacial-like state. Such action entails

88. Mean temperature projections for the late twenty-first century are discussed in an earlier review: Climate Science.

89. Xu et al., "Global Warming," 30, 32. According to this study, the most recent IPCC report, in failing to duly emphasize warming's accelerating rate of advance, recommends certain mitigation strategies that could increase the rate and intensity of warming.

90. Steffen et al., "Trajectories of the Earth System," 8252.

stewardship of the entire Earth System—biosphere, climate, and societies—and could include decarbonization
of the global economy, enhancement of biosphere carbon sinks, behavioral changes, technological innovation,
new governance arrangements, and transformed social
values.[91]

In other words, a "deep transformation" is needed, "a fundamental reorientation of human values, equity, behavior, institutions,
economies, and technologies."[92] This wonderful aspiration amounts
to a world-wide conversion experience, a mass awakening that
transforms all aspects of life. It is a freshened and bigger ecological
version of the utopian projects that haunt the past two centuries
and which include the peacemaking digital fantasia promised only
a few decades ago. As an idea, collective human action is internally
contradictory for neglecting the dark traits that have shaped human interaction, particularly governing entities, since at least the
Nataruk rampage. Collective action of this scope is unfeasible, if
not practically, then psychologically. We could as easily return to
the primeval garden and start again, trusting in a better outcome.

Certain spiritual practices could create sufficient motivation
to pursue practical interventions with the constancy and the degree of self-sacrifice required for some degree of material success.
These practices do not begin with overt action but rather subjugation—subjugation of the impassioned fantasies that have brought
the developed world to its current state of profligacy, confusion,
and aesthetic blight. A "deep transformation" is required, a "fundamental reorientation," but one quite unlike that of the scientists.[93]
It would be signaled, initially, by worldwide outcries of lament,

91. Steffen et al., "Trajectories of the Earth System," 8252.

92. Steffen et al., "Trajectories of the Earth System," 8252, 8258. Basically
the same plan appears in UN Environment, *Global Environmental Outlook*,
18. A plan of comparable scope is recommended in the report commissioned
by the Club of Rome, which speaks of "the initiation of new forms of thinking
that will lead to a fundamental revision of human behavior and, by implica-
tion, of the entire fabric of present-day society" (Meadows et al., *Limits of
Growth*, 190).

93. Steffen et al., "Trajectories of the Earth System," 8252, 8258.

followed by widespread acts of penitence and the adoption of semi-ascetic ways of life on the part of millions of people. From among those so affected, remnant bands would form, herald voices, persons equally charitable and brave. The resulting odds would not legitimize marked optimism in mastering the material aspects of global warming, but many persons will have gained the spiritual means to cope with the fear and physical challenges of a dimming future. A suitably shaped version of old traditions would take form: a spiritual tradition that ensured emotional perseverance and the continuity of transcendent meaning over coming generations.[94]

In Anders's view, the invention of nuclear weapons altered our temporal perspective, our concept and feeling of passing time. This lethal innovation forced us into a new era, which he calls the *Time of the End*. In this kind of end-time, we face "the *naked apocalypse*, that is: the apocalypse that consists of mere downfall, which doesn't represent the opening of a new, positive state of affairs (of the 'kingdom')."[95] "From now on," writes Anders, "we are sentenced to live in a situation whose character cannot change any more: in the 'Time of the End' which can never end but by the end itself, and which will remain the 'Time of the End' even if we succeed in postponing the 'end of Time' from day to day. . . . This character of our epoch will never disappear, for once we have acquired the ability to precipitate the 'End of Time,' we have acquired it once and for all."[96]

The atomic bomb was first tested in 1945, in the state of New Mexico, as part of a federally sponsored project called Trinity.[97] This codename was assigned by Robert Oppenheimer, the director of the Los Alamos Laboratory. In choosing the name, he was influenced by the opening line in the fourteenth of John Donne's

94. For novel social pathways that may thrive in the Anthropocene, see Bennet et al., "Bright Spots," 441–48; Carpenter et al. "Dancing on the Volcano," art. 23. Neither of these articles addresses a spiritual tradition.

95. Anders, "Apocalypse without Kingdom," 1. The italics and the parenthetical material "(of the 'kingdom')" are Anders's.

96. Anders, *Burning Conscience,* 136.

97. US Department of Energy, "Manhattan Project."

Holy Sonnets: "Batter my heart, three person'd God." The geographic place-names of the test site are revealing: the bomb was exploded near the Valley of Fires, due north of Poison Hills, west of Oscura Peak, and within the Journada del Muerto, meaning "deadly journey," or "the journey of the dead," or "the working day of the dead." The Trinity blast launched our journey through death, darkness, fire, and poison. Oppenheimer, a Sanskrit scholar, misquoted Krishna's words to Arjuna when he witnessed the blast: "Now I am Death, the destroyer of worlds." In the *Gita*, the word "Time" (*kalah*) is used rather than "Death": "I am Time, now engaged in laying desolate the worlds, here ready to consume the people."[98] Any trinity in evidence at the blast site was infernal—the reverse of the three-person'd deity, the precise opposite of its incarnation.

Neither Anders nor Korner could have known that global warming would join nuclear war as a comparably dire prospect. And yet the two threats differ in important ways. Atomic warfare is elective and avoidable, but global warming has become inevitable and is worsening. Were carbon emissions halted tomorrow, the global mean temperature would continue to rise, its repercussions cascading through coming millennia. The two threats also diverge at their respective temporal frames. A large-scale atomic war is an all-at-once catastrophe, followed by the creeping noxiousness of radiation poisoning. Its temporal pattern is like a waveform, peaking instantly before subsiding slowly. Global warming, on the other hand, progresses across multiple time frames. Of its vectors of change, some advance gradually, incrementally; others suddenly, as if lurching forward; still others are unpredictable, seemingly chaotic. A marine environment subjected to decades of warming may show relatively minor changes before simply collapsing, as if switched off. In comparison, vegetation in a drought-plagued area may gradually succumb, its range shrinking until only desert remains. The temporal panorama of climate change is complex and millennia-long. God's eye could survey such a scene, but not our eyes. We are tapping at the end of the blind man's cane, hiding fear and bereavement in our feeble effort to change.

98. de Coster, *Bhagavad Gita in English*, 183.

Our time in history is doubly inflected. The grinding down imposed by global warming has been added to the threat of sudden extinction. The claustrophobic state of suspension imposed by the Time of the End is now compounded with the crepuscular fear of inexorable climate change. The coincidence of these temporal frames is like a watch with two faces and one incomprehensible mechanism. Neither timeframe is reversible. We are running in place while moving backward. A certain mood is in question, an entangled set of emotions that forms the subjective milieu of our historical moment. The mindset it creates allows for certain predictions about future cultural change. Two mutually implicated tendencies are in play: to one side is violence, nihilism, and antinomian routs; to the other is the contracting grip of autocratic leaders whose powers increase in tandem with the enrichment of their propaganda and digital outreach. These tendencies evolve toward the respective sociopolitical scenarios of George Orwell and Aldous Huxley. To one side is blithe oppression grounded in pleasure, toys, devices, and entertainment; to the other is hard oppression informed by totalitarian constraints and militarized enforcement.[99] The point is not that either scenario is new or surprising, but that they are present at once, each driving the other to new heights of intensity.

A real-world cataclysm is underway. The facts point to its worsening later this century. Dare we accept the facts, knowing that acceptance is a necessary preliminary to plotting a forward course that proves other than make-shift and temporary? How can the heart acquire vigor and perseverance as we face the coming storm? What can be done within the next few decades that will allow children born after mid-century to acquire a spiritual tradition adequate to their worldly circumstances? The task begins individually before broadening to encompass others. It begins within, before its repercussions are manifest in overt effects. The answer, briefly stated: seek the fear, sadness, and grief of the moment—and see straight the outrage of what has happened—then turn these emotions toward lament, penitence, and worship, and so, in this manner, pass

99. The two scenarios are investigated in detail and depth in Weber, *Political Vindication*.

into the spiritual process of *penthos.*[100] The outlined path is opposed to the passivity of institutional religion and all forms of religious sentimentality. It is not a recommendation for quietism, nor is it a masochistic turn, though retreat and pain are required during the early stages of its application. *Penthos* is an ancient practice, a narrow gate, whose severity and range of transformative effects are comparable to the scope and severity of the physical and emotional challenges to be anticipated as the Anthropocene advances into the final decades of the present century. It is not a solution to global warming; it is a *modus vivendi* and a guarantor directed at the spiritual needs of future generations. The situation is serious. Failing a welcomed knock, the door must be stormed.[101]

In bringing *penthos* to bear, one fights fire with fire. One fire confers safety; the other burns with bitterness and leads to inward collapse. The desirable fire awakens charity, delivers quietness of mind, and safely conveys the traveler through the moral sickliness and emotional brutality that have begun tearing open the surface of civil culture. Grief is inevitable, thus the practice's alternate name—*Tears.* Beyond and intermingled with grief is acceptance, benevolence, and charged intentions toward work, including work for human betterment. The other fire, the one that leads to inward collapse, is the familiar mixture of anger, hatred, and resentment, all in service of masking fear and despair. This fire feeds on the additional fuel of naive fantasies of the technological mastery of the natural order. Later this century, when the coarse voices of primitive mentality have grown louder and more insistent and threatening, spiritual freedom will be of utmost importance. The first fire liberates, the second fire enslaves. Sackcloth is unnecessary, but ashes may be useful.

---

100. For *penthos*, see Bradford, "Mystical Process," 59–104; Ware, "'Obscure Matter,'" 242–54. For a classic work in this area, see Hausherr, *Penthos.* The spiritual path recommended here and elsewhere in the main text can be understood as "interiorized monasticism," as discussed in Evdokimov, *Ages of the Spiritual Life.*

101. For "narrow gate," "knock," and "stormed," see Mt 7:7, 13, 14; 11:12.

"ALL CREATION GROANS"

Certain of the "last things" addressed in eschatological scriptures are now subject to interpretation as material effects of global warming. The leading example is a seemingly chaotic wildness running rampant in the natural order. Nature, it seems, at least Nature as humans experienced it during the preceding geological epoch, is edging toward the brink. Some of the harsh and deadly consequences of climate change have already become obvious. More subtly, a sense of feverish pace and break-neck momentum thickens the air, as if something invisible, pervasive, dangerous, and limitlessly distracting were afoot. Three of the major causes of this disturbing sense are old news: the near-instantaneity of digital communication, the flattening of cultural differences based on globalization, and the trivialization of most scales of value apart from the avarice mandated by neoliberal economics. The sense of marginal control grading into radical change was also apparent to early Christians, who faced the repressive force of Rome, conflict within their ranks, and, most importantly, their Savior's unanticipated death and the prospect of His imminent return. A key passage in this regard is found in Paul's letter to the church in Rome: "We know that all creation groans and is in agony even until now" (Rom. 8:22).[102] He proceeds from this point, charged with hopefulness and excitement. In Paul's view, end-time events were set to occur in the very near future, and in these pressing circumstances he advised "patient endurance" as Christians await the "redemption of our bodies" (Rom. 5:4; 8:25). Their "glory" was ensured—"the glory to be revealed in us"—and this included bodily glorification (Rom 8:18). Because we "share the image of his Son," who is "the first-born of many brothers" and sisters, we are destined to see the fulfillment of Paul's magnificent promises (Rom 8:29).

Paul had glimpsed the coming changes when he envisioned the animate, incorruptible luminosity of Christ during his ecstatic conversion experience while riding to Damascus (1 Cor 15:3–8;

---

102. For this verse and its eschatological setting in Rom 8:18–24, see Blackwell et al., *Paul and the Apocalyptic Imagination.* For Rom 8:22 as a prime text in ecotheology, see Hunt et al., "Environmental Mantra?" 546–79.

Gal 1:11–16; Acts 9:3–9; 22:6–21; 26:12–18). This particular experience was a foretaste of coming events and the precedent for his claims about incipient cosmic rejuvenation. Paul merged his personal mysticism and his eschatological thinking and, in doing so, succumbed to a common risk among mystically inclined spiritual writers. These writers tend to objectify mystical phenomena and assume that the material world will replicate envisioned realities. Their error is an understandable instance of epistemological slippage. For persons with first-hand knowledge, the distinction between visionary reality and the overt material world is a moving target.[103]

In Paul's view, bodily glorification will be paired with an analogous transformation of "the whole created world" (Rom 8:19). The two forms of change are reciprocally related and morally intertwined, and both are pending. The two sorts of entities—our bodies and the earth—are substantially alike and have overlapping destinies; but humans are the dominant causal agents. It is our sin that has corrupted the world and brought all to the point of requiring a Savior's intervention. For Paul, the corruption of the material order, our earth included, corresponds with the bent moral disposition of its human inhabitants. Earth's physical status and the humans' moral status are corollaries, the latter dominating the former. In this troubled situation, Paul called for full adherence to the faith despite the world's turmoil and the burden of corruptible bodies.

Not only us; the world itself is in turmoil. All is groaning, joined in a transformative process of cosmic scope. In a manner that Paul perceived as entirely real, the world and its human inhabitants participate in a single contest whose outcome will be Christ's return and His victory over dark forces:

103. For the experience of the luminous presence of God, see Bradford, *Spiritual Tradition in Eastern Christianity*, 45–92. For epistemological slippage in a modern mystic, see Bradford, "Mystical Process," 135–86. Prayer and meditation routines that elicit mystical experience can prevent such slippage when they are carefully structured (Bradford, "Sacramental Meditation," 1–13). Exaggerated and pathological versions of slippage are found in neuropsychological and psychiatric cases (Bradford, "Therapy of Religious Imagery," 154–80; Bradford "Archetypal Hallucinations," 63–82).

> Indeed, the whole created world eagerly awaits the revelation of the sons of God. Creation was made subject to futility, not of its own accord but by him who once subjected it; yet not without hope, because the world itself will be freed from its slavery to corruption and share in the glorious freedom of the children of God. (Rom 8:19–21)

As the world "groans . . . in agony," we suffer as well, "groan(ing) inwardly while we await the redemption of our bodies" (Rom 8:22, 23). The contest at hand will have one of two outcomes: either "slavery to corruption" or the "freedom of the children of God" (Rom 8:21). Paul is clear about corruption's primary modes of expression: death, decay, and subjection to sin and futility.

The scripture at hand is a bolt of environmental awareness and a prescient instance of eco-mysticism. It is a prophetic word hurled across two millennia into the Anthropocene. The "corruption" and "futility" to which the earth has been subjected can be interpreted as the depredations of anthropogenic climate change and the consequence of the spiritual nescience and dark traits that are presently driving global warming (Rom 8:20, 21). Corruption of this sort is contributing to mass extinction, untold future suffering, and possibly the closing down of a habitable planet. It has introduced "futility," or barrenness, in ecosystems throughout the world. Paul's root metaphor of the gravid mother "groaning in travail" is at once perfect and awful (Rom 8:22). Climate change is the anthropogenic induction of a planetary stillbirth.

Paul's anthropomorphism and sensational language are alien to the materialistic mindset of empirical science and provoke resistance in the postmodern intellect; examples include his vivid descriptions of the glorified body and the agonized, eagerly expectant earth. That one might feel the earth's travail and vicariously suffer its futility are judged to be fantasies of the mind and contrary to fact. Paul's anthropomorphism acquires its correct philosophical context when the theological attribute of absolute transcendence is rejected in favor of panentheistic conceptions of divine participation in material process.[104] Granted this shift in perspective, one

---

104. Clayton and Peacocke, *In Whom We Live.*

can say that Christ-the-Logos suffers the abnormal whittling away of species and the wreckage of previously flourishing natural processes. His propensity for orderly advance has been rejected and is actively fought in the damaging changes we have introduced in the natural order. He is afflicted at our hands. As we once drove nails into His incarnate form, we now nail His planetary display, as if the first murder were not enough to sate the blood lust of the humans.

Paul was convinced of a positive outcome, and his enthusiasm is manifest. In his view, the present struggle is but the "early stages" of a marvelous transformation (Mt 24:8). The "pains of labor," which he felt and reported and which he expected to grow more severe, anticipate our "glorious freedom" and the earth's escape from "its slavery to corruption" (Mt 24:8; Rom 8:21, 22). All things are disposed in eager optimism: "I consider the suffering of the present to be as nothing compared with the glory to be revealed in us. Indeed, the whole created world eagerly awaits the revelation of the sons of God" (Rom 8:18–19). These compelling lines wilt before the realities of global warming. Paul's statement, "[T]he sufferings of the present are as nothing compared with the glory to be revealed," is a disquieting assertion when the opposite is more nearly true: "[T]he sufferings of the present are as nothing compared" with the suffering yet to come (Rom 8:18). And yet his diagnosis, stripped of supernaturalism, is entirely apt: "Creation was made subject to futility, not of its own accord but by" the humans who are damaging the natural order (Rom 8:20). Paul's diagnosis (moral and, odd to say, environmental) is fitting, but the outcome he anticipated is skewed, based as it was on his merging his personal mysticism with the gross realities of material process. The apostle of glorification has proven himself the dark voice of the Anthropocene.

Paul's eschatological event of cosmic glorification is unnatural and improbable. It accords with neither commonsense nor the empirical perspective. But it is not an empty fantasy. It captures a bedrock narrative structure, a deep current within archetypal imagination, the same current that operates throughout eschatological texts, in the mythology of pre-literate cultures, in the wilder reaches of fantasy and dreaming, and in the dystopian content of popular entertainment. As such, it has served human development and cultural evolution from time immemorial, and holds true in ways that bridge psychological reality and material process. The soul is naturally eschatological.[105] Were cosmic glorification to occur, it would be externally imposed rather than produced by natural forces, and its timing and effects would be unpredictable, spontaneous, and as worrying for humans as for the presumptive evil forces that troubled Paul. In other words, it would be strictly messianic. The "groaning" or suffering that Paul described is a different matter, and far less doubtful. It is present, obvious, and worsening, to the extent that a transnational lament will shroud the globe after mid-century. Thereafter, the travail will continue:

> The twentieth and twenty-first centuries, a period during which the overwhelming majority of human-caused carbon emissions are likely to occur, need to be placed in a long-term context that includes the past 20 millennia, when the last Ice Age ended and human civilization developed, and the next ten millennia, over which time the projected impacts of anthropogenic climate change will grow and persist. This long-term perspective illustrates that policy decisions made in the next few years to decades will have profound impacts on global climate, ecosystems and human societies—not just for this century, but for the next ten millennia and beyond.[106]

We have carved our pleasures in the spiraling conch of geological time, and now the animal is emerging—a poisonous, tentacled animal, "a wild beast coming out of the sea," its loveliness turning ugly as it awakens from contentment (Rev 13:1). Paul predicted a positive outcome—a world "freed from its slavery to corruption and sharing in the glorious freedom of the children of God"—but circumstances have turned out otherwise (Rom 8:21).

---

105. I have emended Tertullian's remark, giving it greater theological specificity. He said: "[The] testimony of the soul [is] naturally Christian" (Bindley, *Apology of Tertullian* ch, XVII).

106. Clark et al., "Consequences of Twenty-First-Century Policy," 360–69.

EYE OF THE HURRICANE

The project of climate science entails the gathering of empirical facts and their consolidation and subsequent validation. But something more than facts is needed to grasp the spiritual dimension of climate change. *Meaning* is needed, spiritual meaning, and to this end an epistemology foreign to the project of science is needed; thus the present turn to mystical experience and a vision reported by a personal patient.

This middle-aged man had recently retired from a successful career in business. He had never before sought psychotherapy, and only did so in this instance at his wife's insistence. She made the appointment, she told him what symptoms to report, and she demanded that he describe his experience in Notre Dame Cathedral during their recent Paris vacation. His symptoms included sleep disorder, irritability and temper outbursts, spells of ennui alternating with feelings of intense frustration, and episodes of drunkenness. He had been serious about religious formation as a young man but abandoned such aspirations after joining a college fraternity. He was marginally and conventionally religious, and temperamentally unsuited to reflective spiritual practices. His irreligious mindset had the advantage of shaping a mystical experience of remarkable purity. In his case, mystical afflatus disrupted a mundanely disposed mind, and did so without the embellishments of extraneous religious ideas. He succumbed unprepared, and what he saw and felt was all the more clear.

His words, as he described his vision, have been set in quotation marks in the following mystical account:

> Pondering a near life-sized crucifix in a dim alcove of Notre Dame Cathedral, he succumbed to vertigo. His surroundings began spinning. He stumbled and was barely able to stand, and cried profusely after recovering his equilibrium. When his wife asked about his tears he reported the vision he received while examining the crucifix. What happened was this: He was suddenly and unexpectedly reduced to a spot of consciousness suspended in midair, high within the central column of a

hurricane. He peered downward, and at a great distance he saw the earth's surface. Well above the earth, and centered within the circling storms and clouds, he saw "the real Crucifixion." He said the "real Crucifixion" continues unabated even until now: "I saw him on the cross. It happened once and it continues, and on its basis the world is kept in motion. The real Crucifixion is the center of things," an invisible dynamic of suffering. Were the "real Crucifixion" to cease, the world would "fly apart" and multitudes of people would "panic." I asked what he felt at the time, and he said he was shocked and dismayed to see that the world's coherence is sustained based on something "alive" and "just able to bear the weight." His wife asked why he kept repeating "Impossible!" while he cried. She asked, "What is impossible?" He said it was clear and certain in the moment that God had become a human, and he knew simultaneously that this was "impossible," "inconceivable," totally refractory to human understanding. He felt "stunned" and dismayed. He felt futility because he could not think through what had happened. He had butted against the limit of reasoning.

The experience is notable for its initial vertiginous effect, which disturbed his equilibrium and produced a perception of illusory movement, such that his surroundings began to spin. This spinning sensation and a hurricane's rotational movement have a striking harmony. Subjected to this immense and powerful vision—to the point of succumbing to vertigo—he turned in sympathy with the hurricane. Is vertigo a sensory correlate of his apprehension of God's ineffable nature? Trained mystics have remarked on this particular correspondence.[107] In the present case, the vertigo passed, and his insight about ineffability arrived during a later phase of the vision. The emotional force of the experience's initial phase had propelled the vertigo.[108]

107. For vertigo and ineffability in Diadochos of Photike and Gregory of Nazianzus, see Bradford, "Brain and Psyche," 461–520. For vertigo in Symeon the New Theologian and other manifestations of altered self-embodiment during ascetic practice and mystical experience, see Bradford, *Spiritual Tradition*.

108. The material basis of his vertigo was probably a transient disturbance within the cerebral projections of the vestibular system; see Preuss et al.,

The experience includes four basic visual elements: the hurricane; the "real Crucifixion"; the earth far below; and the man himself—transformed into an epicenter of visual awareness, a disembodied "eye" suspended within the hurricane's inner column, aloft and higher than the "real Crucifixion." The visionary imagery and its movement display several patterns of symmetry, in several spatiotemporal dimensions; the most complex being the hurricane's rotational symmetry. This highly dynamic mystical phenomenon exceeds in effect a three-dimensional display of static imagery. His vision is five-dimensional: not only spread throughout space, but also active in time, and assuming a fifth dimension from its overt spiritual meaning.

Gods have been portrayed as stormy atmospheric systems and other powerful natural forces from time immemorial, well before the Ba'al-inflected Lord of Hosts "traveled on the wings of the wind," riding his storm-cloud chariot (Ps 104:3).[109] Gods of this kind are kings and warriors. They wield regal and military authority, where "authority" means power—as reflected in the destruction wrought when their acts of justice restore righteous order. A hurricane is an organized, massively energetic celestial phenomenon; it functions in the religious imagination as a demonstration of awful justice, tested from without but held in check until it is unleashed in full force at moments of the god's choosing. Extreme weather events, including hurricanes, are increasing in frequency and intensity as the Anthropocene advances. Hurricanes, like other kinds of tropical storms, are vivid symbols of the destructive force of global warming.

The proximity of the "real Crucifixion" to the hurricane's eye enriches the vision's meaning. Christ is not riding or brandishing the storm, nor guiding its approach; He is suffering it. He is not presiding like a judge or enthroned like a king, and He is not a warrior displaying armaments of wind, thunder, and lightning. His fixed

---

"Negative Emotional Stimuli," 411–15. For the temporal structure of a mystical process and its division into sequential phases, see Bradford, "Mystical Process," 135–86.

109. For other examples in Christian scripture, see: Deut 29:19; Job 21:18; Jonah 1:4; Ps 83:15; Is 5:28, 29:6, 66:15; Amos 1:14; Nah 1:3; 2 Peter 2:17.

posture displays agonal suffering and both enforced and voluntary obedience. He is centrally located, encircled by charged might, and passible to the fury of His surroundings. The symbolic resonance of the vision is such that any one interpretation (say, of the hurricane as judicial violence, or the Crucifixion as passive victimhood) beckons its opposite. The vision portrays a coincidence of opposites: a balanced display of the theological attributes of Mercy and Justice. It shows—in concentrated and graphic form—the fundamental religious dynamic of Mercy-and-Justice, with the Crucified embodying mercy and the hurricane administering judgement. These are reciprocally engaged modes of divine action and may reveal a discriminative process within the mind of God.[110] The vision of the "real Crucifixion" shows (in the way that visions *show* rather than *tell*) that Christ's engagement in creation entails His passible witness to the impact of climate change as portrayed in the destructive force of the hurricane. He is fixed in its eye, where He feels and may blunt the toll of global warming.

Have the scales not tipped from Mercy and fallen toward Justice? The mystical account bears on this question where it says: "The world's coherence is sustained based on something 'alive' and 'just able to bear the weight,'" the latter of which can be interpreted in one of two ways: either Mercy is now in process, as reflected in the image of the "real Crucifixion," and will be sustained while Justice is held at bay; or, emphasizing "just able," Mercy cannot be forever sustained and is due to relent—at which point Justice will strike with force. The empirical facts support the second prospect. Certain scriptures provide a modicum of support for the first. Consider the Lord's response to Abraham's pleading on behalf of Sodom: "For the sake of ten, I will not destroy it" (Gen 18:32). Where might ten more be found: in a cave, in a slum, on the street?

---

110. The theological topic of mercy and justice is ancient and dense. Many psalms capture the emotional resonance of the two attributes' reciprocal relationship; for example, "Kindness and truth shall meet; justice and peace shall kiss" (Ps 85:11).

4

The Downward Passage

SHALL WE WAIT ANOTHER century before declaring the failure of the human project, or shall we assume as much and seek the best course forward? Granted the facts, the first alternative is an exercise in temporizing, prevarication, and false naiveté, and an implicit show of faith in the power of *homo faber* to halt climate change through technology. The second alternative, which accords with the facts, is the more reasonable and realistic, and the more demanding in imposing a daunting spiritual task. To meet this task, one must shift the angle of discernment and run more deeply than discursive reasoning, and in this manner, pass downward to see the extravagant forms now coming into play. One must start below, well below, and then work upward in order to envision the coming scene in the deepest imaginal terms; all the while seeking a fitting spiritual response. Rather than the Incarnation, the Resurrection, or some other overworked gospel theme or point of dogma, a different focus is needed—a focus that harmonizes with the material circumstances and spiritual demands of the Anthropocene. The focus and the match are not found on earth or in heaven, and theological abstractions provide only schematic maps. To make the match, a downward passage is needed. A spirit camouflaged in darkness is needed to glimpse the throne that governs coming times. Imagine a self-perpetuating condition of self-erosion that thrives on the hostile impertinence of blocking all ingressive flows of charity. Imagine a balled-up human form made of smoldering, crusted flesh that swats away the Savior's hand as He reaches to touch Hell's last remaining occupant. Imagine a flame that burns brighter after it has consumed all its surrounding oxygen. Such is Hell, a self-subsistent condition of complete alienation from God.[1]

Apart from Hell, I speak of a guide who has made the descent and survived. This is a transparent reference to Christ's descent, His downward passage, the Harrowing of Hell. This segment of His postmortem itinerary is encapsulated doctrinally in the descent clause of early creeds. The history of the clause has been summarized as follows:

> The creeds with a descent clause are originally in Latin, and they do *not* say that Christ "descended into sheol"; they say he descended to "those below" (Latin variants *ad inferos, ad infernos, ad inferna*). It is not the creeds, but the common Christian heritage of Sacred Tradition that specifies this expression to mean the descent of Christ's soul to sheol (or, in Greek, to *hades*). Although the belief was almost certainly expressed using the Greek term, or possibly the Hebrew one (because the Church spread from the East), it was first explicitly codified in Latin creeds. Whatever the exact way in which the article entered the creed, without doubt it is Sacred Tradition that maintains the equivalency among the terms in the three languages afterward.[2]

Sacred Tradition is a living stream, an animate source of personal and collective imagination. Its origins antedate and its development

1. Two works by von Balthasar encourage the image of Hell as a self-subsistent condition of complete alienation from God: *Mysterium Paschale* and *Dare We Hope*.

2. Pitstick, *Christ's Descent into Hell*, 12; also see Yates, "'He descended into Hell,'" 240–50. For the descent in the New Testament, apocryphal literature, patristic writings, and early poetry and liturgy, see Alfeyev, *Christ the Conqueror of Hell*; von Balthasar, *Mysterium Paschale*, 148–88; von Balthasar, *Dare we Hope*, 5–128; Moltmann, *Coming of God*, 250–57.

may abstain from the subsequent constraints of doctrinal formulations. "Long before the descent was to be included in their creeds, starting in the mid-fourth century, Christian storytellers populated the tale with voices erupting from the heavens, from the below ground, and from a cross."[3]

Early portrayals of the downward passage are alike in showing the doors of Hell blown from their jambs, hinges scattered. Shock and dismay attend His entry. A strange violence is in the air. For all concerned, this is a startling scene of sudden awakening, as if they were catapulted straightaway from dreamless sleep into dizzying alertness. Typically, only Christ's back or side is shown; his face is not in view. It is later artwork that portrays full-frontal images, as if a resplendent king were displaying ease and majesty. For the most part, the downward passage is described only by third parties. He moves in silence, a stranger in a land in which two-way communication with those above is futile. The Christian bible has little to say about the downward passage, and subsequent theology not much more. That "he went to preach to the spirits in prison" is inconsistent with early descriptions, if "preach" means speaking (I Peter 3:19).[4] Mere presence is in question, a visionary kerygma that creates blast-furnace cases of light-blindness.

ON SURVIVING HELL

In 1893, a marginally literate Russian soldier arrived at Mt. Athos, where he adopted the name Silouan and eventually became a schema-monk, the most advanced level of monastic formation.[5] Another of the Holy Mountain's workhorse hesychasts, he was devoted to the Prayer of Jesus. He attained automatic recitation of the Prayer within a few weeks and perceived the Taboric light at least once. He was respected for his humility and the constancy of his prayer life. For the most part, his recorded teachings are plain,

3. Frank, "Christ's Descent to the Underworld," 215.

4. The only other pertinent canonical scripture is: "he had first descended into the lower regions of the earth" (Eph 4:9).

5. Sophrony, *Monk of Mount Athos.*

artless, and predictable. His most striking verbal teaching is a lo-
cution he reported receiving from God: "Keep your mind in hell
and do not despair."[6] This message was transmitted in the inspired
setting of a "prayer colloquy," which elevates its significance and
suggests its ongoing relevance.

"Keep your mind in hell and do not despair." Of what manner of hell was Silouan speaking? Did he refer to the killing fields
of World War I? Did he anticipate the small and large holocausts
that began soon after his death in 1938? Silouan was a monk;
geopolitical events were not his focus. His message concerns the
ascetic life, the pursuit of virtue, and the spiritual means of addressing dark times.

The meaning of *hell* is in question. Did Silouan refer to the
self-made hells of particular individuals: yours, mine, or the neigh-
bor's hell, each a personal creation of psychological origin? Or did
he refer to *Hell*, the self-perpetuating condition of complete alienation from God? For Silouan, hell and Hell are adjacent spheres of
experience, with communication running in both directions. The
border dividing Hell and any number of personal hells is porous.
The psyche and the supernatural merge along a common margin.

Personal hells are porous to spiritual factors that originate
elsewhere than in uniquely personal conflicts. This "elsewhere"
has qualities of objectivity, which is clear from its near-identical
expression in any number of personal hells. Review the malign psychological factors described in the ascetic psychology of the major
religious traditions. Similar, often identical, passions are described
in similar ways.[7] The passions form the infrastructure of Hell. Their
sway varies depending on their respective cultural milieu. In the

6. Sophrony, *Monk of Mount Athos.* Sophrony (or his translator) rendered
the saying as: "Keep your mind in hell, and despair not." I prefer the less an-
tiquated syntax of "Keep your mind in hell and do not despair," which reads
more smoothly and conveys the density and concision of an inspired utter-
ance, as occurred in Silouan's "prayer-colloquy": "The Lord Himself taught
me" (116, 117).

7. Comparisons of this nature have been developed between the Evagrian
passions and the hindrances (*nivaranas*) and constructing activities (*sankha-
ras*) identified in Buddhist ascetic psychology; see Bradford, *Spiritual Tradition,* 165–69.

West, lust has lost its earlier burnish. Its marketing has become a tedious charade, a dusty grind, a cartoon with a satin metal finish. Rather than lust, the demon of avarice has taken charge and set about satisfying its appetite at the earth's expense.

"Keep your mind in hell and do not despair." Silouan's message implies that prayerful calls charged with desperation can pass from the psyche and arrive at a destination that encompasses and surpasses the mind. The effect of such calls varies from negligible to marked. That they can have an effect means that despair is avoidable. Their most profoundly affecting point of origin is the margin common to personal hells and the Hell of complete alienation from God. At the margin can be found the hope that counters despair and does so without disguising it. But a guide is needed to ensure safe travel downward, a guide who has made the descent and survived:

> His tapered pennant whips in the wind. He is the wind, he is the captain, the abyss like a garment is his mantle. Peer along his sight lines. Crevices opening, magma rising. Decimated fields, scattered brush fires. Heaps of flammable gadgets, an ear glued to each one. Tables stacked with coins catch fire—the money is melting. Buffeting gusts blow from opposite directions, raising columns of grit. Legs, arms, and tasseled viscera pass through the air like shoals of fish. A leaden sky weighs on pock-marked plains. Bulging tubas pulse in erratic beats. The buzz of punched tambourines sizzles within burlesque tunes pumped from battered accordions. Men with dollar signs tattooed on their foreheads are dancing naked, impervious to the heat, puffing humid clouds of breath-mint sweetness. Spooked children twist hurdy-gurdy cranks. Women clutching headless babies shout in peacock voices while stomping on mounds of daffodils. The scent, the odor, the smell of a carrion race. See the autocracy of Hell. Shuffling crowds gasp and cry, plunge and fall, strangled and coiled, ivy growing from every orifice. Hordes of two-dimensional forms advance in cartoon fashion, prancing with loose-limbed hipness. The ground beneath their feet momentarily becomes transparent. Farther down, I see eroded human forms standing chest-deep in a slurry of ice. Blue sparks of burning

acetylene flash across its surface. Their mouths are black apertures round as circles. I hear wheezy cries and awful moans sustained for seconds, all in monotone. Here, at the margin, is found the hope that counters despair. But a guide is needed to ensure a safe return, a guide who has made the descent and returned. Whispering is heard, the stealth of kindness. His hand on my arm, penalties instantly cancelled. Draperies blue as night unfurl across the horizon. Such lovely stars, and moons waxing into fullness by the second. A line of pennants is seen receding into the distance, an arrow of fluttering lights passing straight through the storm, leveling the anger of history.

Bibliography

Ackerman, Frank, and Elizabeth A. Stanton. *The Cost of Climate Change: What We'll Pay If Global Warming Continues Unchecked*. New York: Natural Resources Defense Council, 2008. https://www.nrdc.org/sites/default/files/cost.pdf.

Adger, W. Neil, et al. "Are There Social Limits to Adaptation to Climate Change?" *Climate Change* 93 (2008) 335–54.

Albrecht, Glenn, et al. "Solastalgia: The Distress Caused by Environmental Change." *Australasian Psychiatry* 15 (2007) 95–98.

Alfeyev, Hilarion. *Christ the Conqueror of Hell: The Descent into Hades from an Orthodox Perspective*. Crestwood, NY: St. Vladimir's Seminary Press, 2009.

Alston, Philip, "UN Expert Condemns Failure to Address Impact of Climate Change on Poverty." United Nations Human Rights, Office of the High Commissioner. June 25, 2019. https://www.ohchr.org/EN/NewsEvents/Pages/DisplayNews.aspx?NewsID=24735&LangID=E.

Alvarez, Ramón A., et al. "Assessment of Methane Emissions from the U.S. Oil and Gas Supply Chain." *Science* 361 (2018) 186–88. https://science.sciencemag.org/content/361/6398/186.

Anders, Günther. "Apocalypse without Kingdom." Translated by Hunter Bolin. 1959. *e-flux journal* 97 (2009) 1–10.

———. *Burning Conscience. The Case of the Hiroshima Pilot, Claude Eatherly, Told in His Letters to Gunther Anders, with a Postscript for American Readers by Anders*. New York: Monthly Review Press, 1962.

Baccini, Alessandro, et al. "Tropical Forests Are a Net Carbon Source Based on Aboveground Measurements of Gain and Loss." *Science* 358 (2017) 230–34. https://pubmed.ncbi.nlm.nih.gov/28971966/

von Balthasar, Hans Urs. *Dare we Hope "That All Men Be Saved"? with a Short Discourse on Hell*. Translated by David Kipp and Lothar Krauth. San Francisco: Ignatius Press, 2014.

———. *Mysterium Paschale. The Mystery of Faith*. Translated by Aidan Nichols. San Francisco: Ignatius Press, 2000.

Banerjee, Neela, et al. *Exxon: The Road Not Taken*. Brooklyn, NY: InsideClimate News, 2015.

Beaugrand, Gregory, et al. "Prediction of Unprecedented Biological Shifts in the Global Ocean." *Nature Climate Change* 9 (2019) 237–43.

Bennet, Elena M., et al. "Bright Spots: Seeds of a Good Anthropocene." *Frontiers in Ecology and the Environment* 14 (2016) 441–48. doi.10:1002/fee.1309.

Bergo, Bettina. "Emmanuel Levinas." *The Stanford Encyclopedia of Philosophy*. Edited by Edward N. Zalta. Fall 2017. https://plato.stanford.edu/archives/fall2017/entries/levinas/.

Berkowitz, Bonnie, et al. "The Terrible Numbers That Grow with Each Mass Shooting." *The Washington Post*. November 6, 2019. https://www.washingtonpost.com/graphics/2018/national/mass-shootings-in-america/;

Bevins, Michael, et al. "Bedrock Displacements in Greenland Manifest Ice Mass Variations, Climate Cycles, and Climate Change." *Proceedings of the National Academic of Science* (Early Edition, July 12, 2012) 1–5. https://sciencenordic.com/denmark-earth-geography/greenland-is-rising-out-of-the-sea/1374434.

Bindley, T. H., trans. *The Apology of Tertullian for Christianity*, Oxford: Parker and Co., 1890. http://www.tertullian.org/articles/bindley_apol/bindley_apol.htm#47.

Blackwell, Ben C., et al., eds. *Paul and the Apocalyptic Imagination*. Minneapolis, MN: Fortress, 2016.

Bourque, François, and Ashlee Cunsolo Willox. "Climate Change: The Next Challenge for Public Health." *International Review of Psychiatry* 24 (2014) 415–22.

Bradford, David T. "Archetypal Hallucinations in Brain Damage." *Quadrant* 28 (1998) 63–82.

———. "Brain and Psyche in Early Christian Asceticism." *Psychological Reports* 109 (2011) 461–520.

———. "Emotion in Mystical Experience." *Religion, Brain and Behavior* 3 (2013) 103–18.

———. "Mystical Process in Isaac the Syrian: Tears, *Penthos*, and the Physiology of Dispassion." *Studies in Spirituality* 26 (2016) 59–104.

———. "Mystical Process in Richard M. Bucke's Experience of Cosmic Consciousness." *Studies in Spirituality* 29 (2019) 135–86.

———. "Sacramental Meditation." *Journal of Pastoral Care and Counseling* 67 (2013) 1–13.

———. *The Spiritual Tradition in Eastern Christianity: Ascetic Psychology, Mystical Experience, and Physical Practices*. Leuven: Peeters, 2016.

———. "A Therapy of Religious Imagery for Paranoid Schizophrenic Psychosis." Edited by M. H. Spero. *Psychotherapy of the Religious Patient*. Springfield, IL: Charles C. Thomas, 1985. 154–80.

Brown, Oli, and Alec Crawford. *Rising Temperatures, Rising Tensions: Climate Change and the Risk of Violent Conflict in the Middle East*. Winnipeg,

Manitoba, Canada: International Institute for Sustainable Development, 2009.

Bultmann, Rudolf. *New Testament and Theology and Other Basic Writings.* Translated by Schubert M. Ogden. Minneapolis, MN: Fortress, 1984.

Burke, Marshall, et al. "Higher Temperatures Increase Suicide Rates in the United States and Mexico." *Nature Climate Change* 8 (2018) 723–29.

Burke, Marshall, et al. "Global Non-Linear Effect of Temperature on Economic Production." *Nature* 527 (2015) 235–39. doi:10.1038/nature15725.

Burke, Marshall, et al. "Warming Increases the Risk of Civil War in Africa." *Proceedings of the National Academy of Sciences* 106 (2009) 20670–74.

Burkert, Walter. *Greek Religion*, Cambridge, MA: Harvard University Press.

Butler, Colin D. "Infectious Disease Emergence and Global Change: Thinking Systemically in a Shrinking World." *Infectious Diseases of Poverty* 1 (2012) 1–5. doi.10.1186/2049-9957-1-5.

Carleton, Tamma A. "Crop-Damaging Temperatures Increase Suicide Rates in India." *Proceedings of the National Academy of Sciences* 11, no. 33 (2017) 8746–51.

Carpenter, Stephen R., et al. "Dancing on the Volcano: Social Exploration in Times of Discontent." *Ecology and Society* 24, no. 1 (2019) art. 23. https://doi.org/10.5751/ES-10839-240123.

Ceballos, Gerardo, et al. "Biological Annihilation via the Ongoing Sixth Mass Extinction Signaled by Vertebrate Population Losses and Decline." *Proceedings of the National Academy of Sciences* 114 (2017) E6089–96. doi.10.1073/pnas.1704949114.

Center for Climate and Energy Solutions. "Climate Basics." https://www.c2es.org/content/extreme-weather-and-climate-change/.

Center for Disease Control and Prevention. "Opioid Overdose: Understanding the Epidemic." n.d. https://www.cdc.gov/drugoverdose/epidemic/index.html.

Christian, D. "The Anthropocene Epoch: The Background to Two Transformative Centuries." In *The Oxford Illustrated History of the World*, edited by Felipe Fernandez-Armesto, 339–73. Oxford: Oxford University Press, 2019.

Chryssavgis, John, and Bruce V. Foltz, eds. *Toward an Ecology of Transfiguration: Orthodox Christian Perspectives on Environment, Nature, and Creation.* New York: Fordham University Press, 2013.

Cigna. *Loneliness and the Workplace. 2020 U.S. Report.* https://www.cigna.com/about-us/newsroom/studies-and-reports/combatting-loneliness/.

Clark, Helen, et al. "A Future for the World's Children? A WHO-UNICEF-Lancet Commission." *The Lancet* 395 (2020) 605–58. https://www.unicef.be/content/uploads/2020/02/childhealth.pdf.

Clark, Peter U., et al. "Consequences of Twenty-First-Century Policy for Multi-Millennial Climate and Sea-Level Change." *Nature Climate Change* 6 (2016) 360–69. https://scholar.harvard.edu/files/dschrag/files/156._consequences_of_twenty-first-century_policy_2016.pdf.

Clayton, Susan, et al. *Mental Health and Our Changing Planet: Impacts, Implications, and Guidance*. Washington, DC: American Psychological Association, 2017. https://www.apa.org/news/press/releases/2017/03/mental-health-climate.pdf.

Clayton, Philip, and Arthur Peacocke, eds. *In Whom We Live and Move and Have Our Being: Panentheistic Reflections on God's Presence in a Scientific World*. Grand Rapids, MI: Eerdmans, 2004.

Climate Action Tracker. "Pledged Action Leads to 2.9°C—Time to Boost National Climate Action." September 19, 2019. https://climateaction tracker.org/publications/time-to-boost-national-climate-action/.

Climate Policy Info Hub. "The Costs of Mitigation: An Overview." *Climate Policy Info Hub*. https://climatepolicyinfohub.eu/costs-mitigation-overview.

ClimaticAnalytics. "Global Warming Reaches 1°C above Preindustrial, Warmest in More Than 11,000 years." n.d. https://climateanalytics.org/nriefing'global-warming-reaches-1c-above-preindustrial-warmestin-more-than-11000years.

Cobb, J. B. *Is it Too Late? A Theology of Ecology*. 1972. Denton, TX: Environmental Ethics Books, 1995. https://digital.library.unt.edu/ark:/67531/metadc52175/.

Collins, John J. "Apocalyptic Eschatology in the Ancient World." In *The Oxford Handbook of Eschatology*, edited by Jerry L. Walls, 40–55. Oxford: Oxford University Press, 2008.

Cooper, Gregory S., et al. "Regime Shifts Occur Disproportionately Faster in Larger Ecosystems." *Nature Communications* 11 (2020). https://www.nature.com/articles/s41467-020-15029-x).

de Coster, Philippe L. *The Bhagavad Gita in English: The Sacred Song*. Ghent, Belgium: Gita Satsang Ghent, 2010.

Cunsolo, Ashlee, and Karen Landman, eds. *Mourning Nature: Hope at the Heart of Ecological Loss and Grief*. Montreal: Queen's University Press, 2017.

Daly, Robert J., ed. *Apocalyptic Thought in Early Christianity*. Grand Rapids, MI: Baker Academic, 2009.

Dupuy, Jean-Pierre. *Economy and the Future: A Crisis of Faith*. East Lansing, MI: Michigan State University Press, 2014.

———. "Enlightened Doomsaying and the Concern for the Future." http://www.ritsumei.ac.jp/acd/re/k-rsc/lcs/kiyou/pdf_24–4/RitsIILCS_24.4pp.7–13DUPUY.pdf.

———. "The Precautionary Principle and Enlightened Doomsaying: Rational Choice before the Apocalypse." *Occasion: Interdisciplinary Studies in the Humanities* 1 (October 15, 2009). http://occasion.stanford.edu/node/28.

Dutkiewicz, Stephanie, et al. "Ocean Colour Signature of Climate Change." *Nature Communications* 10 (2019) 1–13. https://doi.org/10.1038/s41467–019-08457.

Edenhofer, Ottmar, et al. "IPCC, 2014: Summary for Policymakers." *Climate Change 2014: Mitigation of Climate Change. Contribution of Working Group III to the Fifth Assessment Report of the Intergovernmental Panel on Climate Change*. Cambridge, UK: Cambridge University Press, 2014.

Evdokimov, Paul. *Ages of the Spiritual Life* Yonkers, NY: St. Vladimir's Seminary Press, 1998.

Fernandez-Armesto, Felipe. "The Farmers' Empire: Climax and Crises in Agrarian States and Cities." In *The Oxford Illustrated History of the World*, edited by F. Fernandez-Armesto, 106–38. Oxford: Oxford University Press, 2019.

———. "The Mind in the Ice: Art and Thought before Agriculture." In *The Oxford Illustrated History of the World*, edited by F. Fernandez-Armesto, 42–70. Oxford: Oxford University Press, 2019.

Fitzpatrick, Matthew C., and Robert R. Dunn. "Contemporary Climatic Analogs for 540 North American Urban Areas in the Late 21st Century." *Nature Communications* 10 (2019) 1–7. https://doi.org/10.1038/s41467-019-08540-3.

Forster, Piers M., et al. "Latest Models Confirm Need for Urgent Mitigation." *Nature Climate Change* 10 (2020) 7–10. https://doi.org/10.1038/s41558-019-0660-0.

Francis, Pope. *Encyclical letter* Laudato Si' *of the Holy Father Francis: On Care for our Common Hope*. May 24, 2015. http://w2.vatican.va/content/francesco/en/encyclicals/documents/papa-francesco_20150524_enciclica-laudato-si.html.

Frank, Georgia. "Christ's Descent to the Underworld in Ancient Ritual and Legend." In *Apocalyptic Thought in Early Christianity*, edited by Robert J. Daly, 211–26. Grand Rapids, MI: Baker Academic, 2009.

Freedman, Andrew. "A 'Megafire' Measuring 1.5 Million Acres Forms in Australia as Bushfires Merge." *The Washington Post*. January 10, 2020. https://www.washingtonpost.com/weather/2020/01/10/megafire-measuring-15-million-acres-forms-australia-bush-fires-merge/.

Friedlingstein, Pierre, et al. "Global Carbon Budget 2019." *Earth System Science Data* 11 (2019) 1783–1838. https://doi.org/10.5194/essd-11-1783-2019.

Gamble, Clive. "Humanity from the Ice: The Emergence and Spread of an Adaptive Species." In *The Oxford Illustrated History of the World*, edited by Felipe Fernandez-Armesto, 13–41. Oxford: Oxford University Press, 2019.

Gathercole, Simon. "Jesus' Eschatological Vision of the Fall of Satan: Luke 10,18 Reconsidered." *Zeitschrift für die neutestamentaliche Wissenschaft* 94 (2003) 143–216.

Geophysical Fluid Dynamics Laboratory. "Global Warming and Hurricanes: An Overview of Current Research Results." Updated August 15, 2019. https://www.gfdl.noaa.gov/global-warming-and-hurricanes/.

Gulledge, Jay, et al. *The Age of Consequences: The Foreign Policy and National Security Implications of Global Climate Change*. Washington, DC: Center for Strategic and International Studies/Center for New American Security, 2007.

Hamilton, Brady E., et al. "Births: Provisional Data for 2018." *NVSS: Vital Statistic Rapid Release*. Report No. 007 (May 2019). https://www.cdc.gov/nchs/data/vsrr/vsrr-007-508.pdf.

Hasegawa, Tomoko, et al. "Risk of Food Insecurity under Stringent Global Climate Change Mitigation Policy." *Nature Climate Change* 8 (2018) 699–703.

Hasel, Gerard F. *The Remnant: The History and Theology of the Remnant Idea from Genesis to Isaiah.* Berrien Springs, MI: Andrews University Press, 1972.

Hauer, Mathew E. "Migration Induced by Sea-Level Rise Could Reshape the US Population Landscape." *Nature Climate Change* 7 (2017) 321–25. https://osf.io/tdu94/download/.

Hausfather, Zeke. "Climate Modeler Explainer: How 'Shared Socioeconomic Pathways' Explore Future Climate Change." *Carbon Brief.* April 19, 2018. https://www.carbonbrief.org/explainer-how-shared-socioeconomic-pathways-explore-future-climate-change.

Hausherr, Irénée. *Penthos: The Doctrine of Compunction in the Christian East.* Kalamazoo, MI: Cistercian Publications, 1982.

Hawkins, Ed, et al. "Estimating Changes in Global Temperature since the Preindustrial Period." *Bulletin of the American Meteorological Society* 98 (2017) 1841–56. doi.10.1175/BAMS-D-16-0007.1.

Heilig, Gerhard K. "The Greenhouse Gas Methane (CH4) Sources and Sinks, the Impact of Population Growth, Possible Interventions." *Population and Environment* 16.2 (1994) 109–37. https://doi.org/10.1007/BF02208779.

Hinze, Bradford E. "The End of Salvation History." *Horizons* 18 (1991) 227–45.

Horton, Benjamin P., et al. "Estimating Global Mean Sea-Level Rise and Its Uncertainties by 2100 and 2300 from an Expert Survey." *Climate and Atmospheric Science* 3 (2018). https://doi.org/10.1038/s41612-020-0121-5.

Hughes, Terry P., et al. "Ecological Memory Modifies the Cumulative Impact of Recurrent Climate Extremes." *Nature Climate Change* 9 (2019) 40–43.

Hunt, Cherryl, et al. "An Environmental Mantra? Ecological Interest in Romans 8:19–23 and a Modest Proposal for Its Narrative Interpretation." *The Journal of Theological Studies* 59 (2008) 546–79.

Jones, Martin. "Into a Warming World." In *The Oxford Illustrated History of the World,* edited by Felipe Fernandez-Armesto, 71–105. Oxford: Oxford University Press, 2019.

King, Greg A. "The Remnant in Zephaniah." *Bibliotheca a Sacra* (October–December 1994) 414–27.

Klein, Naomi. "Let Them Drown: The Violence of Othering in a Warming World." *London Review of Books* 38 (June 2, 2016) 11–14.

Koh, Lian Pin, et al. "Co-Extinctions of Tropical Butterflies and their Hostplants." *Biotropica* 36 (2004) 272–74.

Körtner, Ulrich H. J. *The End of the World: A Theological Interpretation.* 1988. Louisville, KY: Westminster John Knox Press, 1995.

Kramer, Adam D., et al. "Experimental Evidence of Massive-Scale Emotional Contagion through Social Media." *Proceedings of the National Academy of Sciences* 111 (June 17, 2014) 8788–90. doi.10.1073/pnas. 132004011.

Laffoley, Dan. *Ocean Deoxygenation: Everyone's Problem: Causes, Impacts, Consequences, and Solutions. Summary for Policymakers.* Gland, Switzerland, IUCN Global Marine and Polar Programme. https://portals.iucn.org/library/node/48892.

Lahr, Marta Mirazón. "The Discoveries at Nataruk: Warfare among Hunter-Gatherers from Nataruk, West Turkana, 10,000 Years Ago." In *Africa: The Role of East Africa in the Evolution of Human Diversity* (2016). http://in-africa.org/discoveries-at-nataruk/.

Lahr, Marta Mirazón, et al. "Inter-Group Violence among Early Holocene Hunter-Gatherers of West Turkana, Kenya." *Nature* 529 (2016) 394–98. https://www.nature.com/nature/journal/v529/n7586/full/nature16477.html.

Lamperti, Francesco, et al. "The Public Costs of Climate-Induced Financial Instability." *Nature Climate Change* 9 (2019) 829–33. doi.10.1038/s41558–019-0607–5.

Lancaster, John. "You Are the Product." *London Review of Books* 39 (August 17, 2017) 3–10.

Landrigan, Philip J., et al. "The Lancet Commission on Pollution and Health." *The Lancet* 3.391 (2018) 462–512. http://dx.doi.org/10.1016/S0140–6736(17)32345–0.

Lang, Andrew. *The Homeric Hymns. A New Prose Translation and Essays, Literary and Mythological.* New York: Longmans, Green & Co., 1899. https://archive.org/details/homerichymnsaneoohomegoog/page/n13.

Leadley, Paul, et al. *Biodiversity Scenarios: Projections of 21st Century Change in Biodiversity and Associated Ecosystem Services. A Technical Report for the Global Diversity Outlook 3* (Technical Series no. 50). Montreal: Secretariat of the Convention on Biological Diversity, 2010. https://www.cbd.int/doc/publications/cbd-ts-50-en.pdf.

Lenton, Timothy M., et al. "Climate Tipping Points—Too Risky to Bet Against." *Nature* 575 (November 28, 2019) 592–95.

Levinas, Emmanuel. *Difficult Freedom: Essays on Judaism.* Translated by Sean Hand. Baltimore, MD: Johns Hopkins University Press, 1997.

———. *Ethics and Infinity: Conversations with Philippe Nemo.* Translated by Richard A. Cohen. Pittsburg, PA: Duquesne University Press, 1985.

———. *Totality and Infinity: An Essay on Exteriority.* Translated by Alphonso Lingis. Pittsburg, PA: Duquesne University Press, 1969.

Levine, Naomi M., et al. "Ecosystem Heterogeneity Determines the Ecological Resilience of the Amazon to Climate Change." *Proceedings of the National Academy of Sciences* 113, no. 3 (2016) 793–97. https://www.pnas.org/content/pnas/113/3/793.full.pdf.

Lin, Ning. "Tropical Cyclones and Heatwaves." *Nature Climate Change* 9 (2019) 579–80. https://www.nature.com/articles/s41558-019-0537-2.

Lin, Ning, et al. "Physically Based Assessment of Hurricane Surge Threat under Climate Change." *Nature Climate Change* 3 (2012) 462–67. https://www.nature.com/articles/nclimate1389.

Louth, Andrew. "Eastern Orthodox Eschatology." In *The Oxford Handbook of Eschatology*, edited by J. L. Walls, 233–47. Oxford: Oxford University Press, 2008.

Macrotrends, "U.S. Death Rates 1950–2019." https://www.macrotrends.net/countries/USA/united-states/death-rate.

Martinich, Jeremy, and Allison Crimmins. "Climate Damages and Adaptation Potential Across Diverse Sectors of the United States." *Nature Climate Change* 9 (2019) 397–404. doi.10.1038/s41558–019-0444–6.

McCullough, Lissa. *The Religious Philosophy of Simone Weil. An Introduction.* London: I.B. Tauris, 2014.

Meadows, Donella H., et al. *The Limits of Growth.* New York: New York Universe Books, 1972.

Miller, Mary Ellen, and Karl A. Taube. *An Illustrated Dictionary of the Gods and Symbols of Ancient Mexico and the Maya.* New York: Thames and Hudson, 1993.

Milton, John. *Paradise Lost.* London: Penguin Classics, 2003.

Min, Seung-Ki. "Human Fingerprint in Global Weather." *Nature Climate Change* 10 (2020) 15–16. doi.10.1038/s41558–019-0670-y.

Moltmann, Jürgen. *The Coming of God. Christian Eschatology.* Translated by Margaret Kohl. Minneapolis, MN: Fortress Press, 1996.

———. "Talk-Back Session with Jurgen Moltmann." *The Ashbury Theological Journal* 48 (1993) 39–47.

Mora, Camilo, et al. "The Projected Timing of Climate Departure from Recent Variability." *Nature* 10 (2013) 183–87. doi.10.1038/nature12540.

Mora, Camilo, et al. "Broad Threat to Humanity from Cumulative Climate Hazards Intensified by Greenhouse Gas Emissions." *Nature Climate Change* 8 (2018) 1062–71. https://www.nature.com/articles/s41558–018-0315–6.

Moshagen, Morten, et al. "Measuring the Dark Core of Personality." *Psychological Assessment* (in press). https://darkfactor.org/Moshagen,%20Zettler,%20Hilbig%20-%20Measuring%20the%20dark%20core%20of%20personality.pdf.

Moshagen, Morten, et al. "The Dark Core of Personality." *Psychological Review* 125 (2018) 656–88. http://dx.doi.org/10.1037/rev0000111.

Müller, Christopher John. *Promethianism. Technology, Digital Culture and Human Obsolescence.* Lanham, MD: Rowman & Littlefield, 2016.

National Centers for Environmental Information. "Glacial-Interglacial cycles" (November 21, 2019). https://www.ncdc.noaa.gov/abrupt-climate-change/Glacial-Interglacial%20Cycles.

National Institute of Environmental Health Science. "Air Pollution." Updated February 19, 2019. https://www.niehs.nih.gov/health/topics/agents/air-pollution/index.cfm.

Natural Environment Research Council, "Experiment Earth: Report on a Public Dialogue on Geoengineering", August 2010. https://www.ipsos.com/sites/default/files/publication/1970-01/sri_experiment-earth-report-on-a--public-dialogue-on-geoengineering_sept2010.pdf

Nature Climate Change. "Focusing on Climate Change and Mental Health." *Nature Climate Change* 8 (2018). https://doi.org/10.1038/s41558-018-0128-7.

———. "Storms Ahead." *Nature Climate Change* 7 (2017) 671. https://dio.org/10.1038/nclimate3415.

NOAA. "What is the Difference between a Hurricane and a Typhoon?" National Ocean Service (Jan. 7, 2020). https://oceanservice.noaa.gov/facts/cyclone.html.

Nolan, Connor, et al. "Past and Future Global Transformation of Terrestrial Ecosystems under Climate Change." *Science* 361 (2018) 920–23.

Northcott, Michael. "Girard, Climate Change, and Apocalypse." In *Can We Survive Our Origins?: Readings in René Girard's Theory of Violence and the Sacred*, edited by Pierpaulo Antonelli and Paul Gifford, 287–310. East Lansing: Michigan State University Press, 2015.

Northcott, Michael S., and Peter M. Scott, eds. *Systematic Theology and Climate Change: Ecumenical Perspectives*. London: Routledge, 2014.

Otto, Walter F. *Dionysus. Myth and Cult*. Dallas, TX: Spring Publications, 1981.

Oyama, Marcos Dasuke, and Carlos Afonso Nobre. "A New Climate-Vegetation Equilibrium State for Tropical South America." *Geophysical Research Letters* 30 (2003) 5.1–5.4. https://agupubs.onlinelibrary.wiley.com/doi/epdf/10.1029/2003GL018600.

Palacios, Robert. "The Future of Global Ageing." *International Journal of Epidemiology* 31 (2002) 786–91.

Peerbolte, Bert Jietaert. "The κατέχον/κατέχων of 2 Thess. 2: 6–7." *Novum Testamentum* 39 (1997) 138–50.

Pelikan, Jaroslav. *The Christian Tradition: A History of the Development of Doctrine. Volume 1: The Emergence of the Catholic Tradition (100–600)*. Chicago: The University of Chicago Press, 1971.

Peterson, Gregory R. "Falling Up: Evolution and Original Sin." In *Evolution and Ethics: Human Morality in Biological and Religious Perspectives*, edited by Philip Clayton and Jeffrey Schloss, 273–86. Grand Rapids, MI: William B. Eerdmans, 2004.

Peterson, Michael L. "Eschatology and Theodicy." In *The Oxford Handbook of Eschatology*, edited by Jerry L. Walls, 518–34. Oxford: Oxford University Press, 2008.

Pinker, Steven. *The Better Angels of Our Nature: Why Violence Has Declined*. New York: Penguin Books, 2012.

Pinnock, Clark H. "Annihilationism." In *The Oxford Handbook of Eschatology*, edited by Jerry L. Walls, 462–75. Oxford: Oxford University Press, 2008.

Pitstick, Lyra. *Christ's Descent into Hell. John Paul II, Joseph Ratzinger, and Hans Urs von Balthasar on the Theology of Holy Saturday*. Grand Rapids, MI: William B. Erdmans, 2016.

Population Connection. "Urbanization and the Megacity" (2016). *World PopulationHistory.org*. https://worldpopulationhistory.org/urbanization-and-the-megacity/.

Pörtner, Hans-Otto, et al. "IPCC, 2019: Summary for Policymakers." *IPCC Special Report on the Ocean and Cryosphere in a Changing Climate* (in press). https://report.ipcc.ch/srocc/pdf/SROCC_SPM_Approved.pdf.

Powell, Charles E. "The Identity of the 'Restrainer' in 2 Thessalonians 2:6–7." *Bibliotheca Sacra* 154 (1997) 320–32.

Preuss, Nora, et al. "Negative Emotional Stimuli Enhance Vestibular Processing." *Emotion* 15 (2015) 411–15.

Prozorov, Sergei. "The Katechon in the Age of Biopolitical Nihilism." *Continental Philosophy Review* 45 (2012) 483–503. https://link.springer.com/article/10.1007/s11007-012-9232-y.

Pruetz, Jill D., et al. "Intragroup Lethal Aggression in West African Chimpanzees (*Pan troglodytes verus*): Inferred Killing of a Former Alpha Male at Fongoli, Senegal." *International Journal of Primatology* 38 (January 23, 2017). https://doi.org/10.1007/s10764-016-9942-9.

Raymond, Colin, et al. "The Emergence of Heat and Humidity Too Severe for Human Tolerance." *Science Advances* 6 (2020) 1–8. https://advances.sciencemag.org/content/6/19/eaaw1838.

Reich, David. *Who We Are and How We Got Here. Ancient DNA and the New Science of the Human Past.* Oxford: Oxford University Press, 2018.

Riahi, Keywan, et al. "The Shared Socioeconomic Pathways and their Energy, Land Use, and Greenhouse Gas Emissions Implications: An Overview." *Global Environmental Change* 42 (2017) 153–68.

Rich, Nathaniel. *Losing the Earth: The Decade We Could Have Stopped Climate Change.* London: Picador, 2019.

Richter-Menge, Jacqueline, et al., eds. *2019: Arctic Report Card 2019.* https://arctic.noaa.gov/Portals/7/ArcticReportCard/Documents/ArcticReportCard_full_report2019.pdf;

Riihela, Aku, et al. "Observed Changes in the Albedo of Artic Sea-Ice Zone for the Period 1982–2009." *Nature Climate Change* 3 (2013) 895–98.

Ripple, William J., et al. "'World Scientists' Warning to Humanity: A Second Notice." *BioScience* 67 (December 1, 2017) 1026–28. https://doi.org/10.1093/biosc/bix125.

Rockström, Johan, et al. "Planetary Boundaries: Exploring the Safe Operating Space for Humanity." *Ecology and Society* 14 (2009), art. 32. http://www.ecologyandsociety.org/vol14/iss2/art32/.

Rosenberg, Jeremy. "U.S. Navy Bracing for Climate Change." *NASA Global Climate Change* (March 21, 2012). https://climate.nasa.gov/news/699/us-navy-bracing-for-climate-change/.

Rowland, Christopher. "Eschatology of the New Testament Church." In *The Oxford Handbook of Eschatology*, edited by Jerry L. Walls, 40–55. Oxford: Oxford University Press, 2008.

Rubenstein, Justin. "Induced Earthquakes." (n.d.). United States Geological Survey. https://www.usgs.gov/natural-hazards/earthquake-hazards/induced-earthquakes.

Rushkoff, Douglas. "Survival of the Richest." *Medium* (July 5, 2018). https://medium.com/s/playback/douglas-rushkoff-survival-of-the-richest-eac5601b935b.

Sachdeva, Sonya. "Religious Identity, Belief, and Views about Climate Change." *Climate Science: Oxford Research Encyclopedias*, 1–36. climatescience.oxford.com.

Sala, Nohemi, et al. "Lethal Interpersonal Violence in the Middle Pleistocene." *PLOS ONE* 10 (May 27, 2015), e0126589. https://doi.org/10.1371/journal.pone.0126589.

Sánchez-Bayo, Francisco, and Kris A. G. Wyckhuys. "Worldwide Decline of the Entomofauna: A Review of its Drivers." *Biological Conservation* 232 (2019) 8–27. https://www.sciencedirect.com/science/article/pii/S0006320718313636.

Scheffer, Marten. "Anticipating Societal Collapse; Hints from the Stone Age." *Proceedings of the National Academy of Sciences* 113 (2016) 10733–35. https://doi.org/10.1073/pnas.1612728113.

Scheidel, Walter. *The Great Leveler: Violence and the History of Inequality from the Stone Age to The Twenty-First Century.* Princeton, NJ: Princeton University Press, 2017.

Shakya, Holly, and Nicholas A. Christakis. "Association of Facebook Use with Compromised Well-Being: A Longitudinal Study." *American Journal of Epidemiology* 3 (2017) 203–11. doi.10.1093/aje/kww189.

Sherwood, Steven, and Matthew Huber. "An Adaptability Limit to Climate Change Due to Heat Stress." *Proceedings of the National Academy of Sciences* 107 (2010) 9552–55. https://www.pnas.org/content/107/21/9552.

Silberg, Bob. "Why a Half-Degree Temperature Rise is a Big Deal." *NASA Global Climate Change* (June 29, 2016). https://climate.nasa.gov/news/2458/why-a-half-degree-temperature-rise-is-a-big-deal/.

Silliman, Benjamin. "Climate Change Is a Threat to Military Security." *ForeignAffairs.com.* January 23, 2019. https://www.cfr.org/blog/climate-change-threat-military-security.

Sillmann, Jana, et al. "Climate Emergencies Do Not Justify Engineering the Climate." *Nature Climate Change* 5 (2015) 290–92. https://www.nature.com/articles/nclimate2539.

Simpkins, Graham. "Cyclones Slow Down." *Nature* 558 (2018) 104–07. doi.org/10.1038/s41558-018-0219-5.

Sippel, Sebastian, et al. "Climate Change Now Detectable from Any Single Day of Weather at Global Scale." *Nature Climate Change* 10 (2020) 35–41. https://www.nature.com/articles/s41558-019-0666-7#.

Smedley, Tim. *Clearing the Air: The Beginning and the End of Air Pollution.* London: Bloomsbury Sigma, 2019.

Smith, Matthew R., and Samuel S. Meyers. "Impact of Anthropogenic CO_2 Emissions on Global Human Nutrition." *Nature Climate Change* 8 (2018) 834–39.

Sokolov, Andrei P., et al. "Probabilistic Forecast for the Twenty-First-Century Climate Based on Uncertainties in Emissions (without Policy) and Climate Parameters." *Journal of Climate* 22 (2009) 5175–5204.

Sophrony, Archimandrite. *The Monk of Mount Athos: Staretz Silouan 1866–1938.* Translated by Rosemary Edmonds. London: Mowbrays, 1973.

Spratt, David, and Ian Dunlop. *Existential Climate-Related Security Risk: A Scenario Approach.* Melbourne: Breakthrough—National Centre for Climate Restoration, 2019. https://52a87f3e-7945–4bb1-abbf-9aa66cd4e93e.filesusr. com/ugd/148cb0_90dc2a2637f348edae45943a88da04d4.pdf.

Steelesmith, Danielle L., et al. "Contextual Factors Associated with County-Level Suicide Rates in the United States, 1999 to 2016." *JAMA Network Open* 2 (September 6, 2019). doi:10.1001/jamanetworkopen.2019.10936).

Steffen, Will, et al. "Planetary Boundaries: Guiding Human Development on a Changing Planet." *Science* 347 (February 13, 2015) 1–10. https://science. sciencemag.org/content/347/6223/1259855.full.

Steffen, Will, et al. "Trajectories of the Earth System in the Anthropocene." *Proceedings of the National Academy of Sciences* 115 (2018) 8252–59. http://www.ecologyandsociety.org/vol14/iss2/art32/.

Stephens, D. J. "Eschatological Themes in II Thessalonians 2:1–12." PhD diss., St. Andrew's, 1976. https://research-repository.st-andrews.ac.uk.

Stockholm Resilience Centre, "The Nine Planetary Boundaries." https://www. stockholmresilience.org/research/planetary-boundaries/planetary-boundaries/about-the-research/the-nine-planetary-boundaries.html.

Strasser, Stephan. "Emmanuel Levinas (born 1906). Phenomenological Philosophy." In *The Phenomenological Movement: A Historical Introduction,* edited by Herbert Spiegelberg, 612–52. London: Martinus Nijhoff, 1982.

Thomas, Chris, et al. "Extinction Risk from Climate Change." *Nature* 427 (2004) 145–48. https://www.nature.com/articles/nature02121.

Tonstad, Sigve. "The Restrainer Removed: A Truly Alarming Thought (2 Thess 2:1–12)." *Horizons in Biblical Theology* 29 (2007) 133–51. doi.10.1163/187122007X244066.

UN Environment. *Global Environment Outlook—GEO-6: Summary for Policymakers. Nairobi* (2019). doi.10.1017/9781108639217.

UN Refugee Agency. *Global Trends. Forced Displacement in 2018.* United Nations High Commissioner for Refugees (2019). Geneva, Switzerland.

UNEP Global Environmental Alert Service. "One Planet, How Many People? A Review of the Earth's Carrying Capacity: A Discussion Paper for the Year of RIO+20" (June 2012). https://na.unep.net/geas/archive/pdfs/geas_jun_12_carrying_capacity.pdf.

Union of Concerned Scientists. "Each Country's Share of CO_2 Emissions" (July 16, 2008). Updated October 10, 2019. https://www.ucsusa.org/resources/each-countrys-share-co2-emissions.

United Nations Department of Economic and Social Affairs, Population Division. *Population Prospects 2019: Highlights.* ST/ESA/SER.A/423. https:// population.un.org/wpp/Publications/Files/WPP2019_Highlights.pdf.

———. "World Population Projected to Reach 9.8 Billion by 2015, and 11.2 billion in 2100." (June 21, 2017). https://www.un.org/development/desa/en/news/population/world-population-prospects-2017.html.

———. *World Population Ageing 2017: Highlights*, 2017. http://www.un.org/en/development/desa/population/publications/pdf/ageing/WPA2017_Highlights.pdf.

———. *World Urbanization Prospects 2018*. https://population.un.org/wup/.

United Nations Framework Convention on Climate Change. *Report of the Conference of the Parties on its Twenty-First Session, Held In Paris from 30 November to 13 December 2015*. https://www.un.org/en/development/desa/population/migration/generalassembly/docs/globalcompact/FCCC_CP_2015_10_Add.1.pdf.

US Call to Action. *On Climate, Health, and Equity: A Policy Action Agenda* (2019). The Medical Society Consortium on Climate and Health. https://climatehealthaction.org/cta/climate-health-equity-policy/.

US Department of Energy. "The Manhattan Project: An Interactive History. The Trinity Test." (n.d.). https://www.osti.gov/opennet/manhattan-project-history/Events/1945/trinity.htm.

van Vuuren, Detlef P., et al. "The Representative Concentration Pathways: An Overview." *Climatic Change* 109 (2011), 5–31. doi 10.1007/s10584-011-0148-z.

von Rad, Gerhard. *Old Testament Theology*. Vol. II. Louisville, KY: Westminster John Knox, 1965.

Walls, Jerry L., ed. *The Oxford Handbook of Eschatology*. Oxford: Oxford University Press, 2008.

Ware, Bishop Kallistos. "'An Obscure Matter': The Mystery of Tears in Orthodox Spirituality." In *Holy Tears: Weeping in the Religious Imagination*, edited by Kimberley Christine Patton and John Stratton Hawley, 242–54. Princeton, NJ: Princeton University Press, 2005.

Watts, Nick, et al. "Health and Climate Change: Policy Responses to Protect Public Health." *The Lancet* 386 (2015) 1861–914. doi.10.1016/S0140-6736(15)60854-6.

Weart, Spencer. *The Discovery of Global Warming*. Cambridge, MA: Harvard University Press, 2008. http://www.aip.org/history/climate.

Weber, Michael. *The Political Vindication of Radical Empiricism: With Application to the Global Systemic Crisis*. Anoka, MN: Process Century Press, 2016.

Weeks, Brian C., et al. "Shared Morphological Consequences of Global Warming in North America Migratory Birds." *Ecology Letters* 23.2 (2020) 316–25. https://doi.org/10.1111/ele.13434.

Weinstein, Aviv, and Michel Lejoyeux. "New Developments on the Neurobiological and Pharmaco-Genetic Mechanisms Underlying Internet and Videogame Addiction." *American Journal of Addiction Psychiatry* 24 (2015) 117–25.

White, Aaron M., et al. "Using Death Certificates to Explore Changes in Alcohol-Related Mortality in the United States, 1999 to 2017." *Alcoholism: Clinical and Experimental Research* 44, no. 1 (January 2020) 178–87. https://doi.org/10.1111/acer.14239.

White, Sam. *A Cold Welcome: The Little Ice Age and Europe's Encounter with North America.* Cambridge, MA: Harvard University Press, 2017.

Wikipedia. "2017 Las Vegas Shooting." https://en.wikipedia.org/wiki/2017_Las_Vegas_shooting.

Wilson, Edward O. *The Future of Life.* New York: Vintage, 2003.

Witman, Sarah. "More Earthquakes May Be the Result of Fracking Than We Thought." *Eos,* 99 (February 8, 2018). https://doi.org/10.1029/2018EO091727.

World Health Organization. *Ambient Air Pollution: A Global Assessment of Exposure and Burden of Disease* (2016). https://www.who.int/phe/publications/air-pollution-global-assessment/en/.

World Meteorological Organization. *WMO Statement on the State of the Global Climate in 2019.* Geneva: World Meterological Organization, 2020. https://library.wmo.int/doc_num.php?explnum_id=10211.

World Population Review. "Mass Shootings by Country Population" (October 10, 2019). http://worldpopulationreview.com/countries/mass-shootings-by-country/.

Wuebbles, Donald J., et al. "Executive Summary." In *Climate Science Special Report: Fourth National Climate Assessment.* Vol. I. Edited by Donald J. Wuebbles, David W. Fahey, Kathy A. Hibbard, David J. Dokken, Brooke C. Stewart, and Thomas K. Maycock, 12–34. Washington, DC: US Global Change Research Program, 2017. doi.10.7930/J0DJ5CTG.

Xu, Chu, et al. "Future of the Human Climate Niche." *Proceedings of the National Academy of Sciences* 117, no. 21 (May 2020) 11350–55. www.pnas.org/cgi/doi/10.1073/pnas.1910114117.

Xu, Yangyang, et al. "Global Warming Will Happen Faster Than We Think." *Nature* 564 (2018) 30–32. doi:10.1038/d41586-018-07586-5.

Yates, John. "'He Descended into Hell': Creed, Article, and Scripture. Part I." *Churchman* 102 (1988) 240–50.

Zhang, Xin, et al. "The Impact of Exposure to Air Pollution on Cognitive Performance." *Proceedings of the National Academy of Sciences* 115, no. 37 (2018) 9193–97.

Zhao, Z., et al. "A Hypothalamic Circuit that Controls Body Temperature." *Proceedings of the National Academy of Science* 114 (2017) 2042–47.

Zhu, Chunwu, et al. "Carbon Dioxide (CO2) Levels This Century Will Alter the Protein, Micronutrients, and Vitamin Content of Rice Grains with Potential Health Consequences for the Poorest Rice-Dependent Countries." *Science Advances* 4, no. 5 (2018) 1–8. http://advances.sciencemag.org/.

Zhu, Yunqi, et al. "Molecular and Functional Imaging of Internet Addiction." *BioMed Research International* 4 (2015). http://dx.doi.org/10.1155/2015/378675.